Collins Living History

Pg 126, 127 131; 132 · 133

The People's Century

Britain, Europe and the World in the 20th Century

CHRISTOPHER CULPIN,

PETER FISHER AND FIONA MACDONALD

SERIES EDITOR: CHRISTOPHER CULPIN

Women. Pgs. 18-21, 30-31

MAPS

colour photocopy. Pg 122, 120, 124.

CollinsEducational

An imprint of HarperCollins*Publishers*

Contents

About this book

This book contains all the topics in the core part of the National Curriculum History course at Key Stage 4. They are arranged into seven units.

On the first page of each unit the book makes clear exactly what you are going to find out about and what Key Questions the unit will answer.

Then come two or more pages called 'Setting the Scene'. These give you some of the basic information you will need in order to work through the rest of the unit. You will find these pages useful later if you have to revise this topic for the GCSE examination.

The rest of each unit consists of 'Issues and Enquiries'. These pages provide more detailed information, topic by topic, as well as investigations, simulation activities and discussions. They also include 'Target Questions'. These are aimed at National Curriculum Attainment Targets:

AT1 This is about your knowledge of what things were like in history, how they have changed and why.

AT2 This is about your understanding of how other people explain and interpret the past.

AT3 This is about how we use historical evidence to find out about the past.

There are plenty of other interesting things in the book – but you'll find out about those when you get to them!

The People's Century

The twentieth century is almost over and people are trying to sum it up. One label, used in the title of this book is 'The People's Century'.

In other centuries, History has been dominated by kings, queens, emperors, barons, landowners: the wealthy and the powerful. In this century the voice of the people has been heard much more, as you will see in this book. Many countries have become more democratic, with governments chosen by the votes of all citizens.

Governments have had to take note of the well-being of the people when it comes to making decisions and spending money. Sometimes the change has been achieved through revolutions, where the people have risen up against their traditional rulers and thrown them out. There have been popular independence

▼ The revolution in home entertainment, 1961.

▼ The move towards independence, India, 1931.

movements which have pushed out foreign rulers. Even the wars of this century have involved whole nations, not just a few thousand soldiers.

People have become important economically, as mass production in industry has meant the growth of a mass market, with mass advertising. In many countries, people have become better off than ever, with time and money to spend on holidays, sport, music, entertainment, leisure and travel, all of which had always been beyond the means of ordinary people before.

Such a picture is only one interpretation. Some would argue that this has not really been a 'people's century' at all. Few countries are in fact genuinely democratic; concessions have been made in others, but governments are still in the hands of the wealthy and powerful and the world is still dominated by a handful of rich nations.

So even the title of this book is controversial; as you read it, you will meet other controversies. History is like that. The authors hope that you will be able to use this book to come to your own decision about each controversy, and especially whether this has really been the 'people's century'.

▲ The campaign for votes for women, Britain, 1912.

The world in 1900

▲ SOURCE 1
Spithead Naval Review, 1898. Britain had the largest navy in the world in 1900 and had held this superiority for 100 years.

▲ **SOURCE 2**
The Krupp factory in Essen, Germany, one of the largest steelworks in the world. Weapons for two world wars were built here.

▲ **SOURCE 1**
Spithead Naval Review, 1898. Britain had the largest navy in the world in 1900 and had held this superiority for 100 years.

I n 1900 – if you had money – you could sit at home in London, pick up your telephone and order almost anything grown or made anywhere in the world, asking for it to be delivered to your door that day.

Most Europeans believed that the rest of the world was there to supply European demands and provide a market for European-made goods.

In 1900 the world was dominated by Europe, and the leading nation in Europe was Britain. By 1900 the British Empire was at its peak: it covered nearly a quarter of the globe and included over a quarter of the world's population. It was protected by

◄ SOURCE 3
A miner's family outside their home in Wigan, 1908.

▼ SOURCE 4
Sorting tea at a British tea plantation in Ceylon (now Sri Lanka).

the largest navy in the world, see Source 1.

Britain was not the only nation with an empire. The French Empire covered 6.5 million square kilometres and Portugal, Germany, Belgium, Holland and Spain also held imperial possessions. At the same time, Russia was building up its empire in Asia. Other areas, like Latin America and China, were not actually ruled by European countries, but were completely tied to them through trade just as if they were colonies. Outside Europe, only the USA could match the economic strength of European countries.

However, there were signs that this situation would not last for ever. In British India and French Indochina people were beginning to question imperial rule. They wanted to have the same kind of democracy that British and French citizens

enjoyed at home. At the same time, European rivalries were gathering pace. In 1898 (when the picture shown in Source 1 was painted) Germany began to build up its navy to equal the British fleet. German industry had already overtaken Britain in key areas like steel-making, chemical manufacture and electricity generation, see Source 2. Europeans also began to doubt the relevance of imperial power. What did it mean to the miner's family photographed in Source 3 that Britain ruled a quarter of the world? Socialism, which was gaining strength in every industrial nation, questioned the existing world order.

We now know, as the 20th century draws to a close, how the world changed after 1900. There were two murderous world wars before the century was half way through. New superpowers – the USA and

USSR – emerged. Virtually all the empires of 1900 have vanished and nearly one hundred new nations have been formed. Such events have left European countries, including Britain, uncertain about their futures. You can find out about this changing world order in the 20th century in this book.

However, this book is not just about nations, it is also about people. What was life like for the people in Sources 3 and 4? What changes have there been to their families, homes, leisure time and working life?

Many of the things you will read about are controversial. People often have different views about how and why things happened and which events were most important. This is normal in history. The authors of this book have given their views; we hope that after reading the book you will be able to decide on yours.

Two nations?

Many people have described the Edwardian period as an era of calm before the horrors of the Great War. In fact, as you will find out in this unit, it was a time of upheaval.

Nineteenth century ways of doing things were under attack from all sides. There were new efforts to help the poor. At the same time, women began to mount a serious challenge to the old order.

Key Questions

Was Britain ready for change?

What problems faced Britain in 1900?

How would governments deal with these problems?

Back in 1845 Disraeli had written about what he called the 'two nations' in Britain – the rich and the poor. He said that they were 'formed by different breeding, fed on different food, not governed by the same laws'. Were things still the same at the beginning of the 20th century?

The rich
The little girl sitting on the grass in Source 1 is Vita Sackville-West, aged seven. Source 2 is from an account which she wrote later about life at Knole. These were the rich. They had no need to work. What signs of wealth can you see in these two sources?

Rich people held power, too. The seven sons of Charles, 5th Lord Lyttelton, for example, all held important jobs in politics, education, the Church, the law and the Army. Albert was a clergyman, Neville was Commander-in-chief of British forces in Ireland, George was private secretary to Prime Minister Gladstone, Arthur was Bishop of Southampton, Robert was a lawyer and author of books on cricket, Edward was headmaster of Eton, Alfred played cricket for England and later went into parliament.

The poor
What signs of poverty can you see in Source 3? Poor families lived mainly on bread or potatoes, washed down with tea. They might afford a cheap cut of meat once a week. If we compare this diet with Source 2, or Source 1 with Source 3, we can see that there were still 'two nations', and the figures in Source 4 show the unequal

◄ SOURCE 1
Tea on the lawn at Knole, Sevenoaks, Kent, in 1899. The Sackville-West family with friends.

SOURCE 3 ►
Tea with the family of a low-paid worker in London.

distribution of wealth between them. Casual labourers, like the docker in Source 3, might earn 12/- (60p) a week, but they could be out of work for weeks on end. Farm labourers earned about 13/7 (68p) a week and sometimes also had rent-free housing. In general, workers in industry were better paid, earning about £1.50 a week. The difference between the Edwardian period and Disraeli's time was that the gulf between rich and poor had become unacceptable to many people. Times were changing: you could fly across the Channel, as Blériot did in 1909; you could drive racing cars at 160 kilometres per hour on the racetrack at Brooklands; there were working men in parliament. Perhaps the two nations would come closer together.

> **SOURCE 2**
>
> One just had scones, and egg sandwiches, and pâté sandwiches, and cucumber sandwiches and chocolate cake and walnut cake and coffee cake.... Also there were little plates, with china-handled knives to match, from which people ate jam with toast.... The butler and under-butler and the footmen would move about offering food.
>
> (Food for tea, from *The Edwardians*, by Vita Sackville-West, published in 1930.)

SOURCE 4 ►
The distribution of wealth in Britain in 1905.

Class	Percentage of population	Percentage of national wealth
Upper	1	55
Upper middle	2	25
Lower middle	8	11
Skilled working	56	8
Casual and farm labourers	33	1

Conflict and change in Edwardian Britain

Source 5 shows King Edward VII, who became king in 1901 when he was 59. His mother, Queen Victoria, had reigned since 1837. Edward brought changes to the monarchy. He had many friends and liked being seen in public, whether at the opening of parliament or at the races. As you can see from these two pages, his reign was marked by change and some conflict, in many aspects of life.

▼ **SOURCE 5**
King Edward VII and Queen Alexandra on a Rowntree's chocolate tin. (The date of their Coronation is wrong – it was postponed because Edward was ill.)

Political changes

The gulf between rich and poor was an important issue. In the 1906 election, the Liberals won a huge victory, ending 20 years of almost unbroken Conservative rule. They began a programme to help the poor, the working classes and the elderly, see pages 14 to 15. Labour also achieved their first parliamentary success in 1906 when 29 of their MPs were elected. In the same year women began a militant campaign to get the right to vote, see pages 20 to 21.

	Horse-drawn hansom cabs	Motor-taxis
1904	11,000	2
1911	5,000	6,300

▲ **SOURCE 6**
London taxis, 1904 and 1911.

Time chart

Political

1900 Labour Representation Committee set up to get more working men elected to parliament.
1903 Women's Social and Political Union formed.
1905 Unemployed Workmen's Act.
1906 Liberal landslide win in General Election.
1908 Old Age Pensions Act.
1909 Labour Exchanges Act.
1910 Troops sent in to deal with strikers in Tonypandy, South Wales.
1911 Parliament Act. National Insurance Act.
1912 Home Rule Bill. Ulster Unionists prepare to resist with force.
1914 Outbreak of Great War.

Economic, technological and scientific

1901 Electric trams in many towns, including London, Glasgow and Portsmouth.
1904 All cars to be licensed.
1906 Launch of transatlantic liner the *Mauretania*.
1908 Rutherford explained structure of the atom and won the Nobel prize for chemistry.
1909 Blériot made flight across Channel.
1910 Transatlantic wireless service set up.
1912 *Titanic* sank with loss of over 1,500 lives.
1913 Discovery of isotopes (chemical elements with the same properties but different atomic weights).

Social and cultural

1901 Elgar composed 'Pomp and Circumstance' march ('Land of Hope and Glory').
1902 110,000 attended FA Cup Final between Southampton and Sheffield United.
1907 Rudyard Kipling won the Nobel prize for literature.
1908 Olympic Games held in London.
1910 E.M. Forster's *Howard's End* published.
1911 Roger Fry's exhibition of French post-Impressionist paintings.
1913 D.H. Lawrence wrote his novel, *Sons and Lovers*.
1914 George Bernard Shaw's play *Pygmalion* first performed.

About six men in ten could vote. Some men had more than one vote. There were different ways in which men could qualify for the vote. In the General Election of 1911, the eight million men who voted were able to do so because they belonged to one of the following categories:

Living in a separate house as owner, tenant or through their job	86.1%
Owner or tenant of property worth £2 a year	8.4%
Lodger in rooms worth at least £10 a year (unfurnished)	4.6%
Other, including being a university graduate	0.9%

Apart from women, the main groups excluded from the vote were live-in servants, lodgers in cheap accommodation, the poor and people on the move.

▼ SOURCE 7
Troops entering Liverpool in 1911 to suppress strikes and disorder.

Economic, technological and scientific changes

For many years before 1900 Britain's economic lead over other countries had been slipping. Old industries were declining while new ones, based on modern technology, were growing (pages 16 to 17).

There were important scientific discoveries, but developments in technology, particularly the invention of the petrol engine, made the greatest impact. Cars were still only for the well-off, but 100,000 had been registered by 1909. Motor buses and taxis rapidly replaced horse-drawn public transport, as you can see from Source 6.

Social and cultural changes

More attention was paid to working people, and not just in politics. Popular newspapers were introduced: the *Daily Mail* began publication in 1896, the *Daily Express* in 1900 and the first tabloid newspaper, the *Daily Mirror*, in 1903. Writers like George Bernard Shaw, E.M. Forster and D.H. Lawrence reflected social concerns by making class divisions an important theme in many of their works. New ideas in art, often from abroad, astounded the public.

Violence

Although the changes described above were peaceful, an atmosphere of violence hung over much of this period. Several groups seemed ready to disobey the law to achieve their aims. Militant SUFFRAGETTES set about law-breaking as part of a deliberate campaign. Angry strikers – coal miners and dockers – took illegal action. In some cases, troops had to be called out, see Source 7. Violence almost reached the point of civil war in Ireland in 1914. The majority of the population was Roman Catholic and wanted 'Home Rule' for Ireland, repealing the Irish Act of Union of 1800 and creating an independent parliament in Dublin. In 1912 the Liberals introduced a Home Rule Bill, but Protestant Ulster unionists were bitterly opposed to Home Rule and wanted to keep the union with Britain. Both sides armed themselves for conflict.

*Q*UESTIONS

1   Which events on the timechart affected just the well-off and which affected everyone in the country?

2   Which events were violent and which were peaceful?

3   Why did motor-taxis so rapidly replace horse-drawn cabs?

Who were the poor?

How much money do you really need to live on nowadays? What are the basic necessities? Is a television a basic necessity? What about washing machines, video recorders or holidays? We need to draw a line somewhere and say that anyone below that line is living in poverty.

People lived comfortably in Edwardian Britain on quite a small income. With an income of £3 a week, you could afford a well-furnished house and a servant. People on this income included clerks, shopkeepers, commercial travellers, printers, engineers and teachers. The four passengers on the right in Source 8 would have enjoyed a comfortable income. On the left of the same picture you can see a poor mother with her two children.

In the confident Victorian years many people thought that poverty would gradually disappear as Britain became more and more prosperous. They thought that only the lazy and the drunken would stay poor and that was their own fault. There was no old age pension, no unemployment or sickness benefit. If you could not manage you could be sent to the workhouse, hated and feared by all. But at the end of the 19th century some writers pointed out that poverty, far from decreasing, was still widespread. In 1883, the Reverend Andrew Mearns, a NONCONFORMIST minister, wrote an angry attack against poverty in a book called *The Bitter Cry of Outcast London*.

▼ **SOURCE 8**
'A Scene in the Bayswater Omnibus', a painting by William Joy.

Surveying poverty

Charles Booth, a wealthy shipowner, carried out a systematic survey of London as he did not believe newspaper claims that one in four people were living in poverty. The results were published between 1889 and 1903. He found that dockers and gas-workers earning 21/- (£1.05) a week lived in poverty. Fifteen per cent of London's workers struggled at this level and a further 21 per cent fell below it.

Seebohm Rowntree came from a wealthy Quaker family which owned a chocolate factory in York. He made a careful study of just how little money a married couple and three children in York needed to live on. With an assistant and a secretary, he interviewed 46,754 people in York: two-thirds of the total population. He drew the line between working-class and middle-class people on the basis of whether or not the household had a servant. His results were published in 1901. They showed that a family could survive on 21/8 (£1.08) a week, but they could only manage if they were extremely careful, see Source 9.

Rowntree found that 10 per cent of York's population lived below this poverty line all the time. Another 18 per cent dropped below it regularly, for a number of reasons.

The cycle of poverty

Rowntree described a cycle in which most working people hovered around the poverty line all their lives.
- Young, unmarried people earned decent wages and had no obligations.
- Marriage and children lowered incomes, increased outgoings and pushed people below the poverty line (see Source 10).
- When their children started earning and left home, married couples crossed to the right side of the poverty line again.
- However, illness or unemployment could strike at any time and reduce incomes to poverty levels, see Source 11.
- Old age brought falling earnings to everyone. One third of all old people ended up in the workhouse, having tried to avoid it all their lives.

Living in poverty meant that you did not have enough food, fuel or clothing to keep healthy. Houses were often damp, without a proper water supply or a toilet. Not surprisingly, one child in four born into these conditions did not survive. Rowntree found that in 25 per cent of cases poverty was brought about by the family breadwinner being unemployed, often as a result of old age or illness, and unable to bring in enough money. However, in over 50 per cent of cases the breadwinner was in work, but not being paid enough to keep the family out of poverty. Clearly, the problem of poverty had not been solved, nor was it restricted to the lazy and drunken. More and more people called for the government to do something, as Source 12 shows.

SOURCE 9

A family living on 21/8 (£1.08) must never spend a penny on a rail fare or on omnibus. They must never go into the country, unless they walk. They must never purchase a halfpenny newspaper or spend a penny on a ticket for a concert. They must write no letters to absent children, for they cannot afford to pay the postage. The children must have no pocket money for dolls, marbles or sweets. The father must smoke no tobacco and drink no beer. The mother must never buy herself pretty clothes. Finally, the wage-earner must never be absent from his work for a single day.

(From Rowntree's *Poverty: a study in town life*, 1901.)

SOURCE 11

I went down to the river at Shadwell. No work was to be had there. So I walked eight miles to a cooper's yard in Tottenham. All in vain. I turned to home in despair. By the time I reached Stepney I was dead beat, so I called at a friend's for a rest. They gave me some stew and twopence to ride home. I managed to walk home and gave the twopence to my wife. A man who is out of work for long degenerates. The exposure, the insufficient food have such a bad effect on him that he becomes indifferent whether he gets work or not. Thus he passes from an unemployed to an unemployable state.

(From *The life-story of Will Crooks*, published in 1907. Will Crooks later became a Labour MP.)

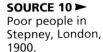

SOURCE 10 ►
Poor people in Stepney, London, 1900.

① Target Questions

1 What was the situation of very poor people in Britain in 1900? Were all poor people drunken or lazy?

2 What were the attitudes towards poverty of Andrew Mearns, Charles Booth, Seebohm Rowntree, Will Crooks and Lloyd George?

3 Suggest reasons for the differences in their attitudes.

4 What motives led people to think about the problem of poverty in Edwardian Britain?

5 Booth and Rowntree were both wealthy men; why did they become interested in the problem of poverty?

SOURCE 12

Listen.... There were 600 men laid off by the Great Western Railway last week. These men had to go out into the streets and starve. There is not a man in the works who does not live in terror of the day when his turn will come. Well, I am against a social order that admits that kind of thing.

(Lloyd George, speaking to Winston Churchill in 1911.)

Socialism

When you studied 'Expansion, Trade and Industry' you saw how industrialisation created two new classes: those who invested money in the new factories and industries (the BOURGEOISIE) and those who worked in them (the PROLETARIAT). SOCIALISTS believed that this system, called CAPITALISM, was unfair. People with money became more wealthy, while people without it did all the work but stayed poor. Socialists wanted working people to take over the government and use its powers to redress the balance between the bourgeoisie and the proletariat.

The man who expressed these ideas most forcefully was Karl Marx (see Source 13). He was a German who fled to London where he wrote his great work *Das Kapital*. His ideas were to change the world in the 20th century.

Socialist movements in Britain

In Britain socialism gained some support in the late 19th century. A socialist society called the Social Democratic Federation (SDF) was formed in 1884: in Source 14 you can see a drawing which appeared on the front page of its newspaper in 1896. Other groups, like the Fabian Society which was founded in 1884, put forward socialist policies. George Bernard Shaw and H. G. Wells were among the founder members of the Fabian Society. In 1893 a group of socialists formed the Independent Labour Party (ILP) and Keir Hardie was their first MP. All these groups wanted to use parliament to pass laws to help working people but none of them had much money or mass support.

'Lib-Labs'

By the end of the 19th century there were some working men in Parliament but they always joined the Liberals and were known as 'Lib-Labs'. Socialists pointed out that the Liberals were a middle-class party and the

▲ SOURCE 14
Drawing by Walter Crane showing the triumph of Socialism, 1896.

SOURCE 13

All history is the history of class struggle. . . . Society as a whole is splitting up into two great hostile camps, two great classes facing each other: the bourgeoisie and the proletariat. The first step in the revolution by the working class is to raise the proletariat to the position of the ruling class, to win the battle for democracy.

(From Karl Marx's *Communist Manifesto*, 1848.)

needs of working people were different from those of the middle classes.

The Labour Representation Committee

The one large working-class organisation with enough funds and members to change things was the trade union movement. Although only a few trade union leaders were socialists, in 1900 the movement did agree to set up the Labour Representation Committee (LRC) to get more working men elected. At first the LRC had little support: only seven unions joined, along with the SDF, the Fabians and the ILP.

Then, in 1901, the Taff Vale Railway Company sued the railway workers' union for loss of income following a strike. The company was successful and won compensation of £42,000. This judgement weakened the unions. They could no longer use their weapon of strike action as they would risk having to pay huge sums of money to employers. More unions joined the LRC to press for a change in the law. In the 1906 election the LRC made a deal with the Liberals not to contest each other in 30 CONSTITUENCIES. Twenty-nine LRC members were elected and began to call themselves the Labour Party.

Liberals and Labour

The Liberals carried out their part of the election deal by passing a number of laws to help working people.

- The Trades Disputes Act, 1906. (This reversed the Taff Vale decision.)
- Miners' shifts were limited to eight hours in 1908.
- The Trade Boards Act, 1909, regulated wages and hours in 'sweated labour' industries (see page 17).
- Labour exchanges (job centres) were set up in 1909.

Many Liberals were uncertain about how to react to Labour's success. Did it mean that there was a big future for the new working-class party and that the Liberals were doomed, as Source 14 suggests? The Liberals had many employers among their supporters: should they risk losing this support by passing laws to help working people? The Liberals and Labour had quite different approaches to poverty, as the table below shows. Soon the two parties were to go in separate directions, see Source 15 and pages 32 to 33.

Andy was a skilled worker in the big factory in his home town. He was well-paid and bought a big house and a car. Then the factory went bust, throwing him and 3,000 others out of work. It is now a year later, he still has no job and heavy hire-purchase debts.

Barry has only worked occasionally in the last ten years. He has no particular skill. He says he has a bad back and takes a lot of time off work when he has got a job. He has five children.

1 *Should these people be paid money by the state while they are unemployed? For how long?*

2 *Would you make any conditions on payment?*

3 *Whose fault is it that they are unemployed?*

4 *Does this matter?*

▼ **SOURCE 15**
Cartoon from 1909. The man on the left is saying: 'Any objection to my company? I'm going your way – and further'.

HOW SHOULD THE STATE HELP THE POOR?	
LIBERALS	**SOCIALISTS**
Approach: people should take some responsibility for themselves. State help should be like an insurance scheme which everyone has to join.	**Approach:** the state should give poor people money out of taxes.
Aims: helping people out at times of crisis.	**Aims:** people need to feel secure at all times.
Criticism of socialists: the socialist solution makes people dependent on the state.	**Criticism of Liberals:** the Liberal solution is only a safety net to help out in emergencies.

The foundations of the Welfare State

Before the 20th century, governments in Britain did not think it was their business to spend money on the welfare of the people. The first government to take on this responsibility was the Liberal government elected in 1906.

Why did the Liberals take these measures?
As we have already seen on page 10, many people in Britain were beginning to raise the issue of poverty. It was the focus of surveys undertaken by researchers like Booth and Rowntree, and was investigated by writers like G. B. Shaw. Teachers pointed out that children were coming to school too hungry and too ill to learn. The army was concerned that nearly half the recruits called up for the Boer War (1899 to 1902) were physically unfit. Other countries, notably Germany but also New Zealand, had already introduced old age pensions and unemployment and sickness payments. The Liberals were worried by the success of the new Labour Party and wanted to show that they could look after working people just as well.

WELFARE FOR YOUNG AND OLD

Children

1906 School meals could be provided. 150,000 meals a day by 1914.

1907 School medical checks started. By 1911 it was clear that one third of all children needed medical treatment.

1908 Children's Act: the 'Children's Charter' set up juvenile courts and BORSTALS.

Old people

1908 Old Age Pensions Act. Pensions were first paid in 1909 for those over 70, at the rate of 5/- (25p) a week and 7/6 (37.5p) for a married couple, see Source 16. The pension was 'means tested': those who had more than 12/- (60p) per week to live on got nothing. Even so some people opposed the idea of a pension paid by right, see Source 17.

Lloyd George and his 'war budget'
Changes in the government in 1908 brought more radical Liberals to power, including Lloyd George (Chancellor of the Exchequer) and Winston Churchill. They were determined to help working people by tackling the basic problems of poverty. This would cost a great deal of money and Lloyd George was determined that the rich should pay. He called his 1909 budget 'a war budget'. He said it was 'for raising money to wage war against poverty'. He raised taxes on the rich, making them pay 1/2d (6p) in the pound on unearned incomes, imposing an extra supertax of 6d (2.5p) on incomes over £5,000 and introducing a tax on land.

◄ **SOURCE 16**
The first payment of old age pensions, January, 1909.

SOURCE 17

We were challenged by the member for Preston (Conservative) who said: 'Would you declare that you are in favour of giving a pension of 5/- (25p) a week to a drunken, thriftless man or woman?'. My reply is very prompt. A man of 70 with nothing in the world is going to cut a pretty shine on 5/- (25p) a week, whether his character be good or bad. Who are you to be continually finding fault?... If a man is foolish enough to get old, and has not been artful enough to get rich, you have no right to punish him for it. They are veterans of industry, people of almost endless toil.

(From a speech by Will Crooks MP.)

The Liberals versus the Lords

These taxes infuriated the Conservatives who were in a minority in the House of Commons but had a majority in the House of Lords. The Conservative leader, Arthur Balfour, described what the Liberals were doing as 'the hasty and ill-conceived offspring of one passionate election'. Other Conservatives said it was 'not a budget but a revolution'. They argued that it was the job of the Lords to block hasty laws until people had time to think and refused to agree to the budget.

The Liberals responded that the Lords were just looking after their own interests as many of them were landowners. The Liberals were confident that they were doing what the people wanted, having won the 1906 election so convincingly, see Source 18. Lloyd George called the House of Lords 'Mr Balfour's poodle: it barks for him. It fetches and carries for him. It bites those he sets it on to'.

The Liberals decided to appeal over the heads of the Lords to the people. In two elections held in 1910 they won a new majority with their allies, Labour and the Irish Nationalists. With this support, the Liberals also introduced a Parliament Act to weaken the powers of the Lords and make parliament more democratic. The new king, George V, stepped in and threatened to create enough Liberal PEERS to defeat the Conservatives if the Lords did not agree to these changes. Under this threat, the Lords backed down and the budget, the Parliament Act and the National Insurance Act were passed, see Source 19.

▲ SOURCE 19
A poster supporting Lloyd George's National Insurance Act, 1911. Lloyd George is sitting on the right.

Review

Look back at the two approaches to poverty in the table on page 13. What approaches did the Liberals adopt to deal with:

- *Old people?*
- *Health?*
- *Unemployment?*

Think about...

1 What is 'means testing'? Was it a fair policy for old age pensions in 1908?

2 Which welfare benefits are means tested today, and which are not? Do you think it is a fair policy now?

3 How successful were the Liberal measures? You should look at the amount of benefit paid, who received the money and for how long, and what happened to workers' families.

SOURCE 18

We are placing the burden on the broadest shoulders. Why should I put burdens on the people? I am one of the children of the people. I was brought up amongst them. God forbid that I should add one grain of trouble to the anxieties which they bear with such patience and fortitude.

(Lloyd George speaking in London's East End in 1909.)

NEW LEGISLATION

The Parliament Act, 1911
- The House of Lords could not block a money bill, such as the budget.
- The Lords could only delay a bill for two years, after which it would become law.
- MPs should be paid a salary (this old CHARTIST demand would allow more working people to enter parliament).

The National Insurance Act, 1911
Part 1 – Health Every employee earning under £160 a year paid 4d (2p) a week. The employer added 3d (1.5p) and the government 2d (1p) to this contribution.

The worker thus got 'ninepence for fourpence'. In return the worker could claim 10/- (50p) a week sickness pay for up to 26 weeks. The scheme was run by insurance companies or unions.

Part 2 – Unemployment This scheme covered two million workers in seven trades. Worker, employer and government each paid 2d (1p) a week. From this fund, workers were entitled to unemployment pay at 7/- (35p) a week for up to 15 weeks a year.

How successful was the British economy?

The Industrial Revolution made Britain a rich country. Food was imported for the rising population and raw materials for the factories. Manufactured goods were then exported throughout the world.

At first Britain had few rivals but, after about 1870, other nations began to compete, especially Germany and the USA (see Source 2 on page 4). This created a 'balance of trade' problem, which remains an important issue in the British economy today. We want to import all the things we need for a good standard of living. We have to pay for these imports by exporting what we make in a competitive world market. The 'balance of trade' is this balance between imports and exports.

In the Edwardian period Britain was extremely successful at increasing exports. Between 1900 and 1913 the value of exports rose from £354 million to £645 million. Imports rose too but not as much. The balance of trade in 1900 was a debt of £160 million; by 1913 the balance of trade was in Britain's favour. The growth in exports was concentrated in products that Britain had sold for decades such as cotton and woollen textiles, coal, machines and ships.

▲ SOURCE 20
A Scottish woman herring-gutter.

Old technology

In the 20th century, Britain was to pay the price for having been the first industrialised nation. Although this had brought many advantages, by 1900 Britain's industrial development was slowed down by old machinery, awkward sites, small factories, tough unions and old-fashioned management. Most people's jobs involved hard, manual labour, see Sources 20, 21 and 22. Source 23 shows how British people were employed in 1911.

Coal

The British economy was still a coal economy: it was used to power trains, ships and thousands of factory steam engines. It was also used to heat homes and to produce gas. Coal production reached its peak, 287 million tonnes, in 1913 and nearly 100 million tonnes of this was exported. The increase was achieved by sinking new pits in areas like South Wales, South Yorkshire and the Midlands, and employing more miners, rather than introducing new technology. In fact, 96 per

◄ SOURCE 21
A coal miner in about 1910.

▲ SOURCE 22
Farm-labourers getting in the hay-harvest.

cent of British coal was still being dug with a pick and shovel as it had been for more than a century. The amount of coal dug by each miner actually fell from 290 to 260 tonnes per year between 1900 and 1913.

Cotton

At the beginning of this century, 86 per cent of British cotton cloth was exported. Cotton production in Britain also increased up to 1914 without any moves towards new technology. Lancashire cotton workers were skilled in using old machinery, and employers were reluctant to invest in new technology. In 1913 only 19 per cent of British cotton was made by the new ring-spinning method which was both faster and cheaper. By contrast, in the USA 87 per cent of cotton was made in this way. Only one British firm used the new Northrop looms, compared with 40 per cent of firms in the USA.

Shipbuilding

In 1913 60 per cent of all the ships made in the world were built in Britain. Shipbuilding took one third of Britain's steel production and employed a huge workforce of manual labourers in the shipyards of the Clyde, Belfast, Liverpool, Barrow and Tyneside.

New technology

By 1900, there were industries which were based on new technology such as chemical production, electricity generation and car manufacture. However, Britain lagged behind other countries in developing these new industries.

HOW THE BRITISH WERE EMPLOYED	
Agriculture	1,250,000
Cotton textiles	605,000
Woollen textiles	223,000
Building	946,000
Coal-mining	874,000
Metal and engineering	1,578,000
Transport	1,424,000
Commerce	790,000
Chemicals	172,000
Food and drink	1,338,000
Domestic service	2,600,000*
*of which 2,100,000 were women	

Women at work

The lines between men and women at work were firmly drawn: some jobs were for men and some for women. Where they did work together, men received higher pay for the same work. In 1910 a male teacher was paid £127 a year whereas a female teacher only received £92. The main employment for women was domestic service, see Source 23. Others worked in their own homes (see Source 27 on page 18) making clothes or other items. They had to put in terribly long hours to make any money. For example, one seamstress was paid 1/- (5p) for 12 blouses, 8d (3.5p) for 12 children's shirts and 2/9 (14p) for 12 nightdresses. It is not surprising that these jobs were called 'sweated labour'.

New technology began to make a difference to women's job prospects: typewriters and telephones were nearly all operated by women, opening up new careers, see Source 24.

▼ SOURCE 24
Women working in a telephone exchange in 1906.

◄ SOURCE 23
British occupations, 1911.

QUESTIONS

1 Which jobs did the new technology of the typewriter and the telephone replace?

2 How has new technology affected typists and telephonists in recent years?

3 The average working week was 59 hours. What is it now? Which days made up the working week in the Edwardian period?

4 How have the jobs of the people in Sources 20, 21 and 22 changed since 1900?

◄ **SOURCE 25**
A family portrait, 1900.

SOURCE 26

Their mother would teach them, by action and by words, that girls and women find it best to submit to husbands and brothers. Their duty was to feed them well, run their errands and bear all burdens save physical ones.

(From the biography of Joseph Ashby, who came from a farm-worker's family.)

Think about...

You have already seen some pictures of women in Edwardian Britain in this book. Look back at Sources 1, 3, 8, 10, 20 and 24 in this unit. As you look at each woman in these pictures, think about the following questions:

1 *What class does she belong to?*

2 *What can the source tell us about the position of women in her class, either in the family or at work?*

3 *What similarities and differences do there seem to be between the positions of women in different classes?*

What was the position of women in Edwardian Britain?

The Victorian family
In the Victorian age men were regarded as the superior sex. They were the breadwinners and the decision-makers. Men were far more likely to receive an education than women, only men could vote in elections, only men could hold important jobs. Women were considered to be the weaker sex. The ideal Victorian wife stayed at home to raise a large family, dependent on her husband and giving way to him on all decisions. However this ideal only applied to upper-class and middle-class families. Working-class wives usually had to go out to work to help support their families.

The Edwardian family
Families in Edwardian Britain were still large (although they were beginning to get smaller) and the father was, in theory, at its head, see Sources 25 and 26. However, in

◄ **SOURCE 27**
This picture appeared in a magazine in 1908 with the caption 'The real head of the household – yet she has no voice in the nation's affairs'. The poster was published as part of the campaign for women to get the vote (see pages 20 to 21). While her baby and drunken husband sleep, the wife toils at her sewing machine.

this issue as in so many others, the Edwardian period was a time when old ideas were being questioned, especially among the middle classes. Marriage was regarded more as a partnership of equals. From 1882 women had been allowed to keep some of their own property when they married (before that everything they owned became their husband's). Contraception was more widely practised, leading to smaller families and so better health and quality of life for middle-class women.

Source 27 is a PROPAGANDA picture which tries to show what the reality of married life could be. The caption suggests that the woman deserves the right to vote more than her drunken husband.

Education and training for women

Some men in the 19th century claimed that studying hard damaged women's brains. Some women were proving them completely wrong. Cambridge University allowed women to study there from 1870 (although at first they had to live 40 kilometres away and tutors went by train to teach them). Medical schools were also opened to women and Elizabeth Garrett Anderson became the first woman to qualify as a doctor in Britain.

The vote

There was one important right which women did not have: the right to vote and stand for parliament. Women began to concentrate their efforts on this cause. They thought that if they could only get into parliament they could then pass laws to put right all the other things which were still unequal. They could change the divorce laws, which said that a man could divorce a woman for adultery but that wives did not have the same right to divorce their husbands. They could deal with unequal pay and sweated labour. They could force parliament to give more attention to health and child welfare. The poster shown in Source 28 illustrates how unjust the situation seemed to be.

Women could already vote in local elections. Women had had the vote in some states in the USA from the 1860s, in New Zealand from 1893. Campaigns for suffrage were gathering strength in several European countries.

Many opposed votes for women. Queen Victoria called giving women the vote a 'mad, wicked folly' and a large number of women agreed with her. Some men claimed that women were emotionally unsound and would be unable to vote sensibly. Others said that as women could not fight for their country, they should not be allowed to vote. Some even argued that if women started getting interested in politics they would stop having children and the human race would die out!

SOURCE 28 ▶
A poster supporting women's suffrage from 1908. The woman in the poster is wearing her university robes.

3 Target Questions

1 Study Sources 25, 26 and 27 and Sources 1 and 3 on pages 6 and 7. Use them to discuss the position of women and men in Edwardian families.

2 Which of these sources do you find most useful for this purpose?

3 What problems do we have in trying to use Source 27 to tell us about Edwardian family life?

4 What uses could we make of Source 27?

5 What does Source 28 tell us about the campaign to win votes for women?

6 Explain some of the problems in trying to use these sources to find out about life in the Edwardian period.

Votes for women

Who took part in the campaign to win votes for women? What support did they have? Why did they fail to win the vote before 1914?

In the late 19th century the campaign for votes for women was organised by the National Union of Women's SUFFRAGE Societies (NUWSS). Its leader from 1897 was Mrs Fawcett, sister of Elizabeth Garrett Anderson. It was a mainly middle-class organisation, although in north-west England many Lancashire mill-workers joined, see Source 29. The tactics of the NUWSS were to write letters to MPs, organise petitions, hold meetings and try to win support by peaceful persuasion. They were called SUFFRAGISTS and had 480 branches in 1914 with 50,000 members.

SOURCE 29 ►
These Lancashire cotton-workers were members of the NUWSS.

F**O**CUS ...*Mrs Pankhurst*

- She was born Emmeline Goulden in 1858, one of ten children in a free-thinking Manchester family.
- She married Dr Pankhurst and together they took an active part in politics.
- She became an effective public speaker.

When her husband died suddenly, Emmeline Pankhurst and her daughters, Christabel and Sylvia, became more involved in the campaign for the vote. In 1903, Emmeline Pankhurst founded the Women's Social and Political Union (WSPU) in Manchester. This organisation arose out of frustration with the tactics of the NUWSS. The WSPU was more militant. It was prepared to use much more forceful tactics, including law-breaking, to keep votes for women in everyone's minds. Members of the WSPU were called suffragettes and they had set up 80 branches by 1914 with about 5,000 members.

▲ Emmeline Pankhurst, photographed in 1913.

The WSPU

Members of the WSPU interrupted political meetings, tried to get arrested, and organised marches and open air speeches, see Source 30. Later they stepped up their actions. By 1908 they were smashing windows of government buildings. They set light to the houses of Liberal politicians who opposed them, chained themselves to railings in Downing Street and slashed paintings.

In Source 31 you can read how Christabel Pankhurst defended these tactics. Mrs Pankhurst once defended herself in court by saying 'We are here, not because we are law-breakers; we are here in our efforts to become law-makers'.

When they were arrested, suffragettes claimed they were political prisoners and not ordinary criminals. They went on hunger strike and were forcibly fed, see Source 32. In 1913 the government passed the 'Cat and Mouse Act', as it was known. This allowed them to release suffragettes who were ill from hunger striking and arrest them again when they were better. The Pankhursts inspired their followers to make daring protests. One suffragette, Emily Davison, was killed when she tried to grab the king's horse in the Derby in 1913.

SOURCE 31

Bad laws made without due authority ought not to be obeyed, but ought to be resisted by every honest man and woman. It is such laws that militant suffragettes have broken.

(Christabel Pankhurst's views on law-breaking.)

SOURCE 32

Then the doctor put down my throat a tube which was something like four feet in length... I choked the moment it touched my throat. Then the food was poured in quickly, it made me sick a few seconds after it was down and made my body and legs double up but the wardresses instantly pressed back my head and the doctor leant on my knees.

(Lady Constance Lytton describing how she was force-fed.)

▲ **SOURCE 30**
Sylvia Pankhurst making a speech in London in 1912.

Why had women not got the vote by 1914?

The problem facing all women who wanted the vote was that this right could only be granted by parliament, which was totally controlled by men. Some leading Conservatives were in favour of votes for women but most of the rest of their party was against it. However, it was the Liberals who were in power from 1906 to 1914 and they were also split on the issue of votes for women. Many Liberals were in favour, but others pointed out that the right to vote had not yet been given to all men and it was generally only more wealthy men who could vote. They argued that if the same criteria were used for women, it would only serve to give more votes to the Conservatives. For these reasons, the Liberal Prime Minister from 1908, Herbert Asquith, was against votes for women. Labour supported an increase in the FRANCHISE to give votes to all men and all women.

At first suffragists and suffragettes worked together. The WSPU moved to London in 1906 and began to target Liberal politicians who opposed them. Soon no leading Liberal was safe to make a speech in public and halls being used for Liberal meetings had to be cleared and checked first. Asquith responded by using delaying tactics. While parliament discussed proposals for votes for women between 1910 and 1912, the WSPU called off its action. However, when all the talk came to nothing, the suffragettes became more militant.

The suffragettes' use of violence led to a split with the NUWSS. Many people were

horrified by the actions taken by suffragettes, especially as women were still supposed to fit the gentle and refined Victorian stereotype. The NUWSS could see all its patient and careful work of persuasion being swept aside by each suffragette outrage. So women had still not got the vote when the First World War broke out in 1914.

Simulation

Get into groups of four. One of you is a suffragist, one is a suffragette, one is a Labour Party member who supports votes for women, and one is a Liberal Party member who opposes votes for women.

Read these pages carefully.

1 *It is 1909 and the Liberals are about to discuss votes for women in parliament. What do the suffragist and the suffragette say to the MPs? What do the MPs say in reply?*

2 *It is 1913, just after Emily Davison's death at the Derby. Now what do the four people say to each other about votes for women?*

The masses

The 20th century has been called the age of the masses. In earlier centuries the majority of the British population counted for very little. The country was ruled by kings, queens and barons or, after 1689, by rich landowners. Most people were too poor to have money to spend and worked such long hours that they had little time for organised sport or leisure activities. They could not read, so there were no books or newspapers written for them.

All this changed after the Industrial Revolution. Factories made goods in such large quantities that they had to sell to more than just the rich. They needed a 'mass market' and used advertising to get their products known to the masses. Examples of advertising from this period can be seen in Sources 33, 34 and 38. Mass public transport systems – tube trains, trams and buses – were developed to move people around the new, huge, teeming cities.

Education and relaxation

After 1884 most men had the vote, so politicians had to take notice of mass opinion. After 1870 every child was taught to read at school. The first popular newspapers were launched: the *Daily Mail* began in 1896 and sold for a halfpenny. It was soon selling a million copies a day. Its owner, Lord Harmsworth, had a slogan: 'explain, simplify, clarify'. He did not try to compete with the long, heavy pages of type in older newspapers like *The Times*. The first tabloid, the *Daily Mirror*, began in 1903 and kept all its stories under 250 words long.

Gradually, people had a little more spare time for mass leisure activities. Organised sport gained a mass following: 450,000 people attended the 32 FA Cup ties in 1908. However, as Source 35 shows, some people criticised the new trends in professional football. People got together to enjoy themselves in a number of other ways, shown in Source 36, 37 and 38. Music halls became popular places of mass entertainment and made the first 'stars', like Marie Lloyd pictured in Source 39, who were known and admired by millions. Another new form of mass entertainment was also just beginning: by 1914 most towns had at least one cinema.

▲ **SOURCE 33**
An advertisement for the District Line tube trains in London, from the early 1900s.

SOURCE 34 ▶
An advertisement for Eno's fruit salts (used to help indigestion) from about 1900.

SOURCE 35

What was once a good healthy sport is now converted into a business. The leagues are a farce: it is only a question of which team has the most money. Teams are called 'Everton', 'Liverpool', 'Blackburn Rovers' and 'Sunderland' but they do not deserve their names for they do not represent the talent of their own town, but merely an alien crew of men bought from all over the country.

(A letter written to the *Daily Express* in 1911. Professional soccer had a huge following and transfer fees of up to £1,000 were paid for players.)

QUESTIONS

1   What evidence is there on these pages that people had more leisure time?

2   What evidence is there that people had more money to spend on leisure activities?

3   What evidence is there of gender differences in the ways people spent their leisure time?

▲ SOURCE 36
Bathers in the sea in 1913.

▲ SOURCE 38
A programme for the 'Palace of Varieties' music hall, from 1901. Music halls offered live entertainment and entry was cheap as the owners expected to make money selling drinks at the bar.

▲ SOURCE 37
A cycling club outing to Yarmouth in 1906. The club seems to be made up of members of the Independent Labour Party.

◄ SOURCE 39
Marie Lloyd (1870–1922) was a music hall star.

23

The Jarrow Crusade

There have been great changes this century in the working lives and the political lives of the British people.

In this unit we shall see that many more people gained the right to vote.

We shall look at changes in the British economy and how these changes affected people's jobs.

We shall compare the ways different political systems tried to deal with economic crisis.

Key Questions

How and why have work opportunities for British people changed in the 20th century?

How have developments in technology affected changes in work?

How effective have various governments been in dealing with changing problems of employment?

How does their effectiveness compare with governments in other countries?

How has the position of women changed this century, in work and in politics?

The successes of the British economy before the First World War, described on pages 16 and 17, did not continue after the war. Unemployment reached one million in 1921 and never fell below that figure until the Second World War broke out in 1939.

Places dominated by old 19th century industries were the most badly affected. A town which suffered particularly was Jarrow, on Tyneside. Jarrow had relied on its shipbuilding and steel industries, so when both these industries closed down, 8,000 people, many of them skilled workers, were thrown out of work. Unemployment in the town in the mid-1930s was running at 68 per cent.

Encouraged by their Labour MP, Ellen Wilkinson, the townspeople decided to march the 500 kilometres to London to ask the government for help. A group of 200 men was chosen to set off on the Jarrow Crusade in 1936, see Source 1.

Britain was not the only country to suffer serious unemployment between the wars. People looked abroad to see what measures other

◄ SOURCE 1
Marchers on the Jarrow Crusade in 1936.

SOURCE 3 ►
Factories in Cumbernauld, Scotland, photographed in 1968.

▲ SOURCE 2
This dam was built in Tennessee, USA in 1933 under President Roosevelt's 'New Deal'.

Time chart

1918 Representation of the People Act.

1926 General Strike.

1928 Votes for women on same basis as men.

First Five Year Plan in Soviet Russia.

1929 Wall Street Crash.

1933 Roosevelt comes to power in USA.

Hitler comes to power in Germany.

1936 Jarrow Crusade.

1947–1949 Nationalisation of coal, electricity, gas, railways and steel.

1969 Voting age lowered to 18.

1973–1974 Energy crisis: inflation reaches 30 per cent.

1977 Sex Discrimination Act.

governments were taking. Some admired Hitler's Nazi government in Germany, others were impressed by Stalin's 'five year plans' in the USSR. However, neither of these countries were democracies. Many people believed that the policies for rebuilding the economy outlined in US President Roosevelt's 'New Deal' (Source 2) could be usefully copied in Britain.

The Jarrow Crusaders and many others felt that government spending on worthwhile schemes would get the economy going again. The petition signed by the Jarrow Crusaders was presented to parliament by Ellen Wilkinson. The government listened, but did nothing.

Since 1945, however, Labour and Conservative governments have tried to deal with areas of high unemployment. Several New Towns have been built in depressed areas and new industries have been encouraged to set up factories in these regions in order to provide jobs, see Source 3.

25

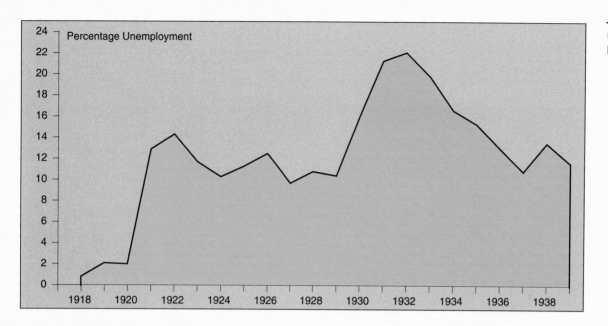

◄ SOURCE 4
Unemployment in Britain between 1918 and 1938.

Britain in the world economy, 1918 to 1939

Britain's economic success in the 19th century and even up to 1914 had relied on exports (see page 16). This meant that Britain had to compete with other industrialised nations in selling goods around the world. From the end of the First World War Britain found it increasingly difficult to stay competitive, particularly in the old industries like cotton, coal, shipbuilding, iron and steel.

What were the reasons for this? During the First World War many countries had been cut off from British suppliers, and so had gone elsewhere. Other countries like Japan began making their own iron and steel. They used very cheap labour (often operating British-made machinery) so their products were competitive. As you saw on page 16, British industry had been slow to take on new technology. So now many of Britain's industries were old fashioned, with high running costs which made it hard for them to compete. In addition, world trade in the 1920s and 1930s was at a low ebb. Europe was in chaos after the First World War. Although there was slow recovery towards the late 1920s, the Wall Street Crash in 1929 brought world-wide depression, see pages 36 to 37. Britain could only win a smaller slice of a shrinking market.

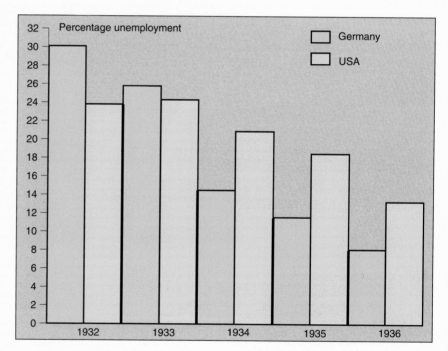

Unemployment
After a short boom between 1918 and 1920, when firms were catching up with orders put off during the war, unemployment never fell below one million (see Source 4). As early as 1921 36 per cent of shipbuilding workers and 37 per cent of iron and steel workers were unemployed. In the worst years, 1932 to 1933, unemployment reached nearly three million. (Some estimates, taking uninsured workers into account, put the figure at 3.75 million.) Source 5 shows how Britain's unemployment and recovery compared with other countries.

▲ SOURCE 5
Unemployment in Germany and the USA between 1932 and 1936.

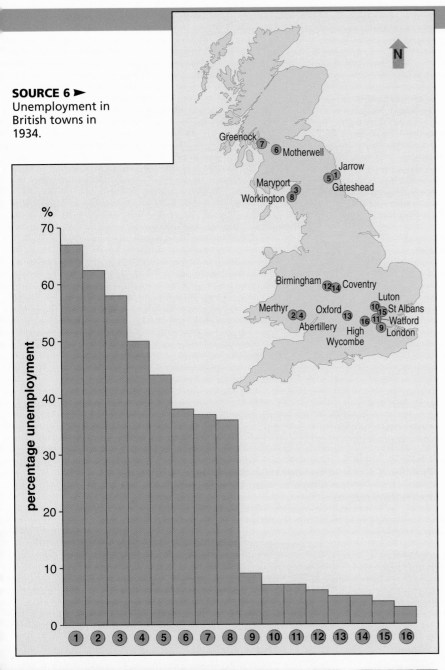

SOURCE 6 ▶
Unemployment in British towns in 1934.

percentage unemployment — % / 70 / 60 / 50 / 40 / 30 / 20 / 10 / 0

① ② ③ ④ ⑤ ⑥ ⑦ ⑧ ⑨ ⑩ ⑪ ⑫ ⑬ ⑭ ⑮ ⑯

Greenock ⑦ ⑥ Motherwell
Jarrow
⑤ ①
Maryport ⑤ ①
Gateshead
③
Workington ⑧

Birmingham ⑫⑭ Coventry
Luton
Merthyr ② ④ Oxford ⑩
⑬ ⑮ St Albans
Abertillery ⑯ ⑪ Watford
High ⑨ London
Wycombe

A varied picture

The figures in Source 4 conceal regional variations in unemployment which are revealed in Source 6. Unemployment was very high in areas like south Wales, Scotland and northern England where old industries were concentrated. However there were jobs available in other areas, especially in the south east.

'New' industries manufacturing cars, electrical goods, artificial fibres, aircraft, chemicals and scientific instruments were actually expanding. The production of artificial silk, for example, rose by 16 per cent from 1923 to 1935, for electrical goods and cars the increase was 10 per cent and for chemicals it was 5 per cent during the same period.

Location of the new industries

As Source 7 shows, these new industries were actually taking on workers. The total number of employees in new industries rose from 370,000 in 1907 to 745,000 in 1924 and to 914,000 in 1930. Owners of these industries preferred to set them up in south-eastern England or the midlands. There was no need to be near coal fields or ironworks. Instead it was important that these industries were near their customers. So factories were built close to large cities, often along major roads, like the famous Hoover factory on the Great West Road on the outskirts of London. You can read more about the contrast between areas of traditional, heavy manufacturing and the new industries on pages 42 and 46.

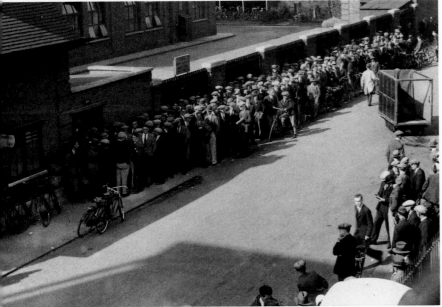

◀ **SOURCE 7**
Unemployed men queuing outside an electrical goods factory in Hayes, Middlesex, which was taking on workers in 1932.

QUESTIONS

1 Why did Britain find it hard to compete internationally after 1918?

2 How far was Britain responsible for its economic and industrial difficulties? Give reasons for your answer.

3 How does the information in Source 6 help to explain Source 7?

CHANGES TO THE VOTE, 1918 TO 1969

- The Representation of the People Act of 1918 extended the vote to all men over the age of 21 (except peers, criminals, lunatics and, until 1924, CONSCIENTIOUS OBJECTORS). Women who were over 30 and already eligible to vote in local government elections or married to men who could vote in these elections could also now vote in general elections. The number of people with more than one vote was reduced under the terms of this Act to 227,000.

- In 1928 all women got the vote, on the same basis as men.

- In 1969 the voting age for both men and women was lowered to 18.

Voting in Britain

We have already seen that in 1900 Britain was far from being a fully democratic country (see page 9). There were seven different ways of qualifying for the vote and people had to live at the same address for 12 months in order to get on the electoral register.

In a city like Glasgow, for example, where workers moved about a good deal looking for jobs, only 52 per cent of men could vote. Over the whole country only about six men in ten could vote. On the other hand about half a million men had more than one vote as they qualified in more than one way.

All this was swept away in 1918 with a new, simpler franchise. It resulted in the greatest increase in the number of voters in British history, from eight million to 21 million (13 million men and eight million women). Male voters were still in a majority. It was one man (although not one woman) one vote. The reasons for this are discussed on page 30.

In spite of some hostile jokes (see Source 8) women began to play their part in politics from 1918. In 1928 the franchise was changed to give women the right to vote on the same basis as men and 5.5 million more women got the vote. The question of who should have the right to vote in Britain seemed to be settled for ever. But 41 years later, in 1969, the franchise was widened still further to include everyone over 18, adding three million more voters.

"WHAT'S THE DISTURBANCE IN THE MARKET-PLACE?"

▲ **SOURCE 8**
A cartoon from *Punch* magazine, December 1918. This cartoon tells you more about the cartoonist than about women voters. One of the men is telling the other, 'it's a mass meeting of the women who've changed their minds since the morning and want to alter their voting papers'.

▲ **SOURCE 9**
Students demonstrating in London, 1968.

The voting age was lowered to 18 for a number of reasons. Some people felt that if you could make your own decision to marry at 18 and fight for your country at 18, then you should be allowed to vote. It was widely believed that the student demonstrations of the late 1960s (see Source 9) arose out of young people's anger and frustration at being excluded from politics.

Proportional representation

Voting in a British election is simple: you put a cross opposite the name of the person you want to vote for on the voting slip (see Source 10). But this simple system can produce results which many people find unsatisfactory and undemocratic. Take this imaginary result:

    Candidate A 24,000 votes
    Candidate B 22,000 votes
    Candidate C 20,000 votes

Candidate A would be elected, but a total of 42,000 people voted for somebody else. How can their views be heard? The British system, called 'first past the post', suits a two-party system, see Source 11. For this reason the main parties, who benefit from the system, have been reluctant to change it. However, there are people who do not support any of the main parties: are their views simply to be ignored? As well as representing the majority, a democracy is also supposed to protect minorities.

Today, many other countries, including most of western Europe, have a system of proportional representation (PR). PR was nearly adopted in Britain in the sweeping changes of 1918, and support for it increased in the 1970s and 1980s. Some of the advantages and disadvantages of the two systems are shown in the table below.

Key	Figures show number of elected MPs		
☐ Conservative	☐ Liberal		☐ Others
☐ Labour	☐ Irish Nationalist		

Date	Elected Government			
1906	400	157	83	30
1910	275	273	82	40
1910	272	272	84	42
1918	478 Coalition Government	229 Opposition		
1922	345	142	116	12
1923	191	258	159	7
1924	419	151	40	5
1929	288	260	59	8
1931	554 National Government	52		9
1935	431	154		20 / 11
1945	393	213		12 / 22
1950	315	298		9 / 3
1951	321	295		6 / 3
1955	344	277		6 / 3
1959	365	258		6 / 1
1964	317	304		9
1966	363	253		12 / 2
1970	330	287		6 / 7
1974	301	297	23	14
1974	319	277	26	13
1979	339	269		11 / 16

◄ **SOURCE 10**
Voting slips like this are used in British elections.

Counterfoil
No.

VOTE FOR ONE CANDIDATE ONLY

1	**CHAMBERLAIN**
	Neil Chamberlain
	25A Hurst Road, Clapham, London, SW4 8AP
	The Labour Party
2	**PETITT**
	Trevor Petitt
	57b Francis Street, Victoria, London SW1V 8GD
	Liberal Democrat
3	**VANCE**
	Terry Vance
	Ground Floor, 204 Hill Road, Surbitton, Surrey, KT5 8TY
	Conservative Party Candidate

▲ **SOURCE 11**
Government and parties 1906 to 1979.

FIRST PAST THE POST	PROPORTIONAL REPRESENTATION
Voting is simple.	It is fairer: more people's views are represented in parliament.
It creates strong governments with clear majorities.	It protects minority views.
PR would lead to the growth of lots of small parties, which would result in coalitions and therefore unstable government.	It prevents extremist governments from forcing through policies when they only have minority support.

QUESTIONS

1 What sexist joke is the cartoonist making in Source 8?

2 Do you think 18 is the right age to be allowed to vote?

3 There are various PR systems. Find out how voting systems are organised in other countries.

4 Which system of voting do you favour?

Women, work and politics

How did the First World War change women's opportunities in work and politics?

The story of 'votes for women' seems to have a simple, happy ending. In the First World War women did valuable war work, see Source 12. As a reward, they were given the vote in 1918. Newspaper billboards proclaimed 'The nation thanks the women'. Women had achieved equality at last.

But was it really like that? It is true that 1,345,000 more women were employed in 1918 than had been in 1914, but there was no real equality. Women were paid less and usually did traditional female tasks such as nursing, cleaning and cooking.

The change in working patterns during the war years was purely temporary. When the men came home from the trenches they wanted their jobs back, as the speakers in Source 13 found. In France women also worked hard for the war effort, but they didn't get the vote in 1918.

The question of whether women should vote had got mixed up with the question of whether all men should vote. During the war, an all-party conference was held and agreed to accept 'one man one vote', see page 28. With the issue of male voting out of the way, a system of voting for women could be worked out.

Women were allowed to vote after 1918 if they could already vote in local government elections or if they were married to a local government voter. In any case, they had to be over 30, so the young MUNITIONS workers photographed in Source 12 would not have been able to vote in 1918. The Act produced an electorate which was 60 per cent male and only 40 per cent female. Many women who campaigned for the vote before the war expected that equality and freedom would soon follow the vote. Were their hopes justified?

Women at work

The Sex Disqualification (Removal) Act was passed in 1918, opening up more jobs for women. The writer of Source 14, however, was too enthusiastic. Although there were women in the occupations she mentions, many jobs were still closed to them. High unemployment in the inter-war years meant that there was opposition to women working at all and they were often exploited as cheap labour. Women usually had to give up their jobs when they got married.

▲ SOURCE 12
Women workers filling shells in a munitions factory in the First World War, 1917. Most of these women did not get the right to vote in 1918 as they were under 30.

SOURCE 13

We asked if they could find us a job in the house, where the buses are parked, or cleaning them. Anything. But no, it had to be men. It was for the men – well, that was natural wasn't it?

(Women tram conductresses ask to carry on working after the war.)

SOURCE 14

How the historian of 100 years ago would be confounded if he could return and see the world of women today! He would find women engineers, architects, lawyers, doctors, dentists, vets, librarians, journalists, scientists and tax inspectors. Today 14,000 women are employed in banks, over 80,000 in Government departments, as sales managers, buyers in the big stores, skilled workers in factories.

(Woman writer in the *Daily Telegraph*, 1937, describes women in various jobs in the 1930s.)

▲ SOURCE 15
A woman car driver from 1930.

Women in politics

There were 17 women candidates in the 1918 election. Lady Astor became the first woman MP to take her seat in 1919. After the 1918 Act it became clear that giving the vote to women would not upset traditional politics. There was therefore little opposition to giving votes to all women at 21 in 1928. Margaret Bondfield became the first woman cabinet minister in 1929. But women found it hard to get selected as candidates, and harder to get elected. Even in the best of the inter-war elections, in 1931, only 4.8 per cent of candidates were women, and only 15 became MPs, which was a mere 2.4 per cent of the total. In the 1935 election, the number of women MPs dwindled to nine.

Women's personal lives

There was some increase in women's personal freedom in these years. It became acceptable for women to go out alone, smoke in public or drive a car (see Source 15). A new generation of young women, nicknamed 'flappers', emerged in the 1920s. They flaunted their new freedoms and followed new fashions for short skirts and hairstyles, quite shocking to those brought up in Edwardian times. Young women were also allowed to meet and socialise with men more freely. However, in spite of these outward signs of greater freedom for women, rules were still strict. Most 'nice girls' waited to be introduced to a man before talking to him and sex before marriage was out of the question.

Marie Stopes published a book called *Married Love* in 1918 in which she set out to educate women about sex. Marie Stopes was also a pioneer of birth control, although she met strong opposition. In 1923 the Matrimonial Causes Act allowed women to divorce their husbands on grounds of adultery. (Husbands had had this right for many years.)

1 Target Questions

1 **How did the First World War change women's opportunities at work between 1914 and 1918?**

2 **How far did the war make a lasting change to women's opportunities:**
   • *at work*
   • *in politics*
   • *in their personal lives?*

3 **Did votes for women in 1918 improve opportunities for women?**

Where did the Liberals go wrong?

Why was there political instability between the wars?

If you look at Source 16, you will see that in 1906 the Liberals had 400 MPs. By 1924 they were clearly the third party, behind the Conservatives and Labour. What can have gone wrong?

Were the Liberals out of date?

The Liberal Party's roots went back to the 19th century. They were the party of high principles, freedom and the commercial middle classes. Under Asquith, Prime Minister from 1908 to 1916, and with Lloyd George and Winston Churchill as ministers, they had passed some important laws on welfare (see pages 14 to 15). But, as we saw in unit 1, by 1914 they were not sure if they wanted to be a working-class party and they had disappointed many women over the vote. They were also unsure about how to deal with Ireland and how to cope with the demands of the First World War when it broke out in 1914.

Was Lloyd George to blame?

In 1916 Lloyd George became Prime Minister in a COALITION GOVERNMENT with the Conservatives to run the war more vigorously. He was very successful, but the Liberal Party was split between those who supported Lloyd George and those who went into opposition, led by Asquith. When the war ended, Lloyd George kept the coalition going. He was a popular politician, but his support in the House of Commons came from 335 Conservative MPs and only 133 coalition Liberals. He was a Liberal leader dependent on Conservative support, so when the Conservatives refused to back him any longer in 1922, he fell from power.

The drift from Liberalism

The party was split and many Liberal voters were disillusioned. Lloyd George had failed in his promise to provide a country 'fit for heroes to live in'. He had failed to deal with unemployment. Many Liberal voters were worried by the rise of Labour and the power of the trade unions. They turned away from the Liberals to the Conservatives.

	Liberal MPs	Labour MPs
1906	400	30
1918	133 coalition 28 independent	63
1922	62 coalition 54 independent	142
1923	159	191
1924	40	151
1929	59	288
1931	68	52
1935	20	154

◄ **SOURCE 16**
The number of elected Liberal and Labour MPs between 1906 and 1935.

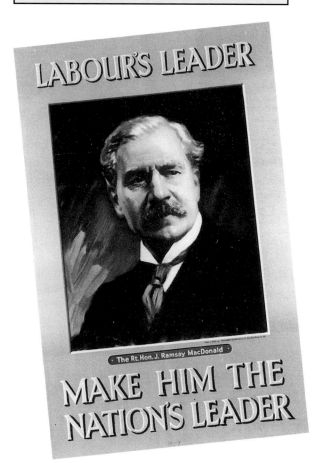

▲ **SOURCE 17**
Ramsay MacDonald, the leader of the Labour Party. This is an election poster from 1924.

The rise of Labour

The extension to the franchise in 1918 did not automatically benefit Labour. Although the working class made up a huge part of the electorate, many still supported the Liberals. Many others had no faith in political parties but put their hopes in the trade unions. Trade union membership grew from 2.5 million workers in 1914 to 6.5 million in 1920. As the economy became more depressed, industrial conflict between management and the unions intensified: in 1921 86,000 working days were lost through strike action. The clash between working people and their middle-class employers was fierce. Working people no longer wanted to vote for a middle-class party and turned to Labour. The rise in Labour support can be seen in Source 16.

The first Labour Government

In the election of 1923 the Conservatives won 258 seats, Labour 191 and the Liberals 159. The Labour leader, Ramsay MacDonald (see Source 17) was asked to form the first Labour Government with Liberal support. As Source 18 shows, many of its members were working men. Although the party was in power for only ten months, Labour proved that it was quite capable of government. Liberal support fell dramatically in the next election (see Source 16).

The National Government

Stanley Baldwin's Conservative government took control at the 1924 General Election. The government dealt with the General Strike of 1926 (see pages 34 to 35) and in 1927 passed the Trades Disputes Act to prevent such strike action taking place again by making it illegal. At the 1929

SOURCE 18

As we stood waiting for His Majesty, amid the gold and crimson magnificence of the Palace. I could not help marvelling at the strange turn of fortune's wheel which had brought MacDonald the starveling clerk, Thomas the engine driver, Henderson the foundry labourer and Clynes the mill hand to this pinnacle, beside the man whose forbears had been kings for so many generations. We were making history.

(J.R. Clynes describes the first Labour Government in 1924.)

election, in the aftermath of this, there was a swing towards Labour. Labour gained 288 seats and was the largest party. Ramsay MacDonald became Prime Minister again. He was immediately forced to deal with an economic crisis. In 1931, as the crisis deepened, the only remedy he could offer was cutting the dole, but this was unacceptable to many of his Labour colleagues. MacDonald felt the crisis was serious enough to form a National Government in coalition with the Conservatives, see Source 19. MacDonald believed he was putting his country before his party, but the Labour Party felt he was putting the bankers before the people and expelled him. Only 13 Labour MPs went with Ramsay MacDonald into the National Government, along with 473 Conservatives and 68 Liberals. The National Government won the General Election of 1931 and the Labour Party went into opposition, with just 52 elected MPs.

Target Questions

1

1 *What reasons were there for the decline of the Liberals?*

2 *Do you think it was all Lloyd George's fault for splitting the party in 1916?*

3 *In what ways did the rise of the Labour Party cause the decline of the Liberals?*

4 *In what ways did the decline of the Liberals cause the rise of the Labour Party?*

5 *What do you think was the most important reason for the decline of the Liberals? Explain your choice.*

SOURCE 19 ►
An election poster for the National Government from 1931.

33

The General Strike

Was the General Strike an industrial dispute or was it a threat to elected government?

Of all workers in Britain, the miners had the toughest time. In the early 20th century many workers, particularly miners, were attracted by the ideas of SYNDICALISM. Syndicalists were socialists who gave their support to trade unions rather than political parties, see Source 20. Syndicalists used strike action as their weapon. They believed that a general strike, involving all working people, would bring the country to a halt and make the government powerless. These ideas fuelled the fierce strikes in the years just before the First World War, see page 9. In 1913 the unions of miners, railwaymen and other transport workers formed the 'Triple Alliance'. They agreed that a dispute in any one industry would bring all workers in the alliance out on strike in support.

During the First World War the mines were run by the government. The miners liked this arrangement and they wanted it to continue after 1918. However, as we have already seen on page 32, Lloyd George was dependent on Conservative support in parliament so he handed the mines back to private owners. This caused bitter resentment among the miners.

After the war, the export price of coal fell from £4 a tonne to below £1 a tonne by 1925. Private mine owners proposed cuts in miners' wages and even longer hours in an attempt to save profits. The miners' leader, Arthur Cook, responded with the defiant slogan, 'Not a minute on the day, not a penny off the pay'. The Triple Alliance came out on strike in support of the miners. The government bought time by subsidising miners' wages for nine months, but what was going to happen when the nine months were up?

SOURCE 20

There should be one organisation to cover the whole mining industry in Great Britain. This organisation shall carry out political action completely independent of all parties, to seize whatever advantage it can for the working class.... Alliances should be formed to bring all workers into one union, to work for the taking over of all industries by the workers themselves.

(Adapted from a pamphlet called 'The Miners' Next Step', published in 1912.)

▲ **SOURCE 22**
Food convoy leaving London docks, May 1926. You can read two different descriptions of this incident in Source 23.

◄ **SOURCE 21**
Waterloo Station, 4 May 1926.

Other unions in the TUC promised that they would join a general strike. They sympathised with the miners and feared for wages in every industry. However, they were certainly not syndicalists, but moderate trade unionists trying to look after their members.

Stanley Baldwin's Conservative government was determined not to give in to a general strike, which it saw as an attack on the elected government. It set up the Organisation for the Maintenance of Supplies (OMS) and drafted in volunteers to keep things running in the event of a general strike.

The strike and its aftermath

The government subsidy for miners' wages ran out in May 1926. Negotiations to avert a general strike failed. On 3 May miners, railwaymen, transport workers, builders, chemical workers, printers, engineers, gas workers and shipbuilders all came out on strike: four million workers in all. Workers in essential services, such as health, water and sewage, were not called out. Although the OMS kept a few trains and buses running, the country was virtually at a standstill, see Source 21. Violent incidents were very rare, but the government still called in troops and armoured vehicles to unload imported food, see Source 22.

Both sides printed their views in rival newspapers: the *British Gazette* put forward the government's case, while the *British Worker* spoke for the TUC, see Source 23. The government said the strike was an attack on the constitution. Despite the views of some strikers (see Source 24), the TUC insisted that it was not.

The OMS could not keep the country running for ever. The strikers might have won if they had gone on, but after only nine days the TUC called off the strike. It was clear that the government was not going to give way. The TUC did not like being accused of attacking the constitution and feared that the situation could turn violent. Only the miners' strike action continued.

The general strike left a legacy of bitterness among miners and some other workers. It also influenced the unions in directing their support away from syndicalism towards the Labour Party which won the next general election in 1929.

> ## SOURCE 23
>
> A long line of motor lorries swinging into Hyde Park showed that strikers had suffered an early defeat in their attempt to starve London. The convoy looked like a victorious army.
>
> (*British Gazette*, 10 May 1926.)
>
> I learnt from one of the dockers that about 150 tons of meat had been taken overnight from one of the ships and was now being moved with this unnecessary display of force. The men, whose normal work is to handle thousands of tons of such cargoes each day, lined the streets with arms folded, smiling and chatting, waving a greeting to the soldiers.
>
> (*British Worker*, 10 May 1926.)

SOURCE 24 ►
Strikers' cartoon, 1926. The elephant is saying 'Ooh! I must be careful not to tread on THAT!!!'

2　　Target Questions

1 Give examples of facts and opinions from Source 23. Does Source 22 support either of the views in Source 23?

2 A 'The General Strike is a direct challenge to government.... An effort to force upon 42 million British citizens the will of less than 4 million.... It is a direct hold-up of the nation to ransom.'
   British Gazette.

   B 'The TUC does not challenge the constitution. The sole aim is to secure for the miners a decent standard of life. It is engaged in an industrial dispute.'
   British Worker.

   Which view do you think is a more accurate description of the issues involved in the General Strike?

3 Which sources here might be used to support either view A or view B?

4 Why did the *British Gazette* and the *British Worker* put forward these views?

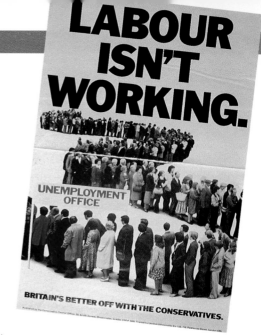

The Great Depression

Source 25 shows a campaign poster from the 1979 General Election. It used the fear of unemployment to win votes. Indeed the Conservative Party did win the election; their victory demonstrated that economics could bring about political change. In the same way, the Wall Street Crash of 1929 and the Great Depression that followed were economic events which brought political change to many countries.

▲ SOURCE 25
A Conservative Party General Election poster from 1979.

What was the Wall Street Crash?

By the 1920s the USA had become the world's most powerful industrial nation. Business boomed. Sales of new mass produced consumer goods soared. Higher wages and increased spending power meant that greater numbers of Americans could share in these boom times. Many of them took advantage of hire purchase spending. The decade was known as the 'roaring twenties'.

Millions of investors began to buy SHARES on the STOCK EXCHANGES hoping to gain a share in the expected profits of successful companies. The biggest stock exchange in the USA was on New York's Wall Street.

Throughout the 1920s the economy was growing. Shares bought for $50 in 1921 were worth over $200 by the middle of 1929. In 1928 America's newly elected President Herbert Hoover appeared confident about America's economic future. He boasted about US productivity, wage levels and spending power which were all higher than in European countries.

However, as Source 26 suggests, there were danger signs. First, the gap between rich and poor was widening: the top 5 per cent of all Americans earned 33 per cent of the nation's income. Black Americans and rural Americans were missing out. The boom depended on selling, but many Americans were too poor to buy. Second, many people had borrowed money to buy shares. As long as prices were going up, these loans could be easily repaid. But if prices started to fall, the boom would suddenly collapse. That is just what happened.

In 1929 there was concern on Wall Street

▲ SOURCE 26
A German cartoon from 1927 attacks the rich financiers' disregard for the poor while they themselves are on the brink of a crash.

that share prices were too high, so shares were sold. By October 1929 panic had set in. Millions tried to sell their shares, even at a loss. Between 24 and 28 October over 16 million shares were sold and $10 billion were lost. This was twice the amount of all the currency in circulation in the USA.

The Wall Street Crash had a knock-on effect as the diagram below shows. Everyone, both the rural poor and the urban rich, felt its effects. The roaring twenties, which began with such optimism, ended with millions of Americans living on the breadline; some of them are pictured in Source 27. Unemployment soared from 1.6 million in 1920 to 4.3 million in 1930 and 12 million by 1932.

President Hoover believed that the economic situation would correct itself and so did nothing to intervene. The population was dissatisfied with his laissez-

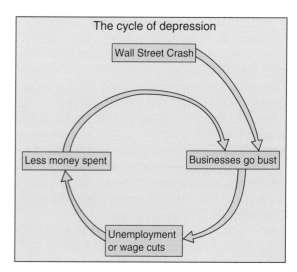

The cycle of depression

Wall Street Crash

Less money spent

Businesses go bust

Unemployment or wage cuts

◄ SOURCE 27
Destitute people from Tyronza, Arkansas queuing for food aid in 1931.

faire attitude and in the 1932 Presidential Election turned to the DEMOCRATIC candidate, Franklin Roosevelt, to offer a way out. Roosevelt promised strong government action to fight the Depression and he won the election.

The Depression

The Great Depression was a world-wide disaster. In Europe, Germany's economy was very fragile. In 1919 Germany lost territory and industrial production and also had to pay £6,600 million in REPARATIONS to its wartime enemies. By 1923 there was 'hyper-inflation' in the country and many Germans lost their jobs and savings. The situation was only saved in 1924 when the Dawes Plan arranged US loans to Germany. The German economy revived and some stability was achieved. However when the Wall Street Crash brought crisis in the USA these loans were recalled. Over £50 million of gold and currency were withdrawn from Germany and unemployment rose from just under two million in 1928 to over six million in 1932.

Desperate Germans lost faith in democracy and turned to extreme parties – the COMMUNISTS and the National Socialists (NAZIS). Support for the Communists rose from 54 seats in the German parliament in 1928 to 77 in 1930. The Nazis increased their power from 13 seats to 107. What was the appeal of Hitler and the Nazis? Hitler offered work for the unemployed and food for the hungry masses. Herr Neisse's experiences described in Source 28 were typical of many. By 1933 the Nazis were the biggest single party and Hitler became Germany's leader.

As US and German investment was

SOURCE 28

Herr Neisse ... had fought in the Great War.... In the disastrous months of 1923 his savings and hopes all vanished overnight ... suddenly ... nothing. Then came 1929 ... leaving a trail of bankruptcies and suicides. He joined an army of six million unemployed ... Communism didn't appeal ... he had always worked for the better off ... he just wanted to belong somewhere. National Socialism [Nazism] was more like it. He began to go to party meetings ... a party member by 1931, he was given a job.

(Memories of a conversation between Christobel Bielenberg and her gardener in 1939.)

withdrawn from the London Stock Exchange, the British economy also declined. The international trade which the British economy had depended on was now in collapse. You can read about the effects of this on page 42. France, Japan, Eastern Europe and Australia all felt the effects of the Depression. By 1933 there were probably 30 million people unemployed world-wide.

QUESTIONS

1   *Explain the reasons why the US economy of the 1920s seemed strong but had underlying weaknesses.*

2   *What were the economic effects of the Wall Street Crash in the USA and Germany?*

3   *What were the political effects of the crash in the USA and Germany?*

4   *How did economic change cause political change? Choose either the USA or Germany to write about in your answer.*

Governments and the Depression

How did different governments respond to the problems of the Depression?

The 1930s were years of crisis in many countries as political leaders struggled with the problems of their economies. We shall start by comparing the USA and Germany. Both were suffering from severe depression and unemployment; both had new leaders in 1933 (Roosevelt in the USA and Hitler in Germany).

Roosevelt's New Deal

Roosevelt had won the 1932 Presidential Election on the promise of a 'New Deal'. Within his first one hundred days as president he introduced a series of measures which laid the foundations for his New Deal. He set up several new government organisations. The AAA (Agricultural Adjustment Act) helped farmers. The NIRA (National Industrial Recovery Act) encouraged workers and employers to work together on fair conditions of work. Goods produced under this scheme could carry the 'Blue Eagle' tag. The FAP (Federal Arts Project) commissioned hundreds of unemployed artists as part of the New Deal, see Source 29. The PWA (Public Works Administration) and WPA (Works Progress Administration) spent government money on large 'public works' schemes creating jobs in building schools, hospitals, roads and harbours. One of the most ambitious schemes was the TVA (Tennessee Valley Authority). Government money was used to revive the whole area, one of the most depressed in the USA. Dams were built to provide water for navigation, irrigation and hydro-electric power generation (look at Source 2 on page 25).

The New Deal did have a significant impact on unemployment, yet four years after Roosevelt came to power, nine million Americans were still unemployed. As Source 30 makes clear, Roosevelt's measures were based upon principles of democracy. In contrast to Hitler's methods, none of Roosevelt's policies involved compulsion. The Wagner Act of 1935 gave every US worker the right to join a trade union. In

◄ **SOURCE 29**
Paul Kelpe was one of hundreds of unemployed artists given work by the Federal Arts Project. Kelpe produced this painting in 1934, it is called 'Machinery'.

SOURCE 30

" These fine changes have not come about by compulsion... they have been debated and discussed [by those] participating in the processes of their government. No farmer was forced to join this conservation movement. No workman was compelled to labour there... for less than a rightful wage. No citizen has lost a single one of these human liberties we prize so highly in this democracy. "

(Roosevelt speaking about the TVA in September 1940.)

1935 the US Supreme Court declared the NIRA unconstitutional, a decision which Roosevelt had to accept.

Hitler's methods

Hitler's methods of reducing unemployment by massive government spending on public works schemes were remarkably similar to those used by Roosevelt in the USA. Like Roosevelt, Hitler adopted strong and decisive policies. However, there the similarity ends. People who did have jobs in Nazi Germany lost their rights over pay, working conditions and hours. Unemployed people were placed on various Nazi work schemes but they were given no choice about the type or location of the work. Unemployment did indeed fall dramatically from six million in 1933 to 2.5 million in 1936 and one million by 1938. For many Germans, these signs of economic recovery justified Hitler's

HITLER'S 'BATTLE FOR WORK'

Re-armament. Despite the restrictions imposed by the Allies after the First World War, increasing numbers of German workers were employed in factories making aircraft, tanks and warships.

Military service. Compulsory military service was introduced in 1935 to employ millions in the armed services.

Labour service. A compulsory National Labour Service was started: all men aged between 18 and 26 had to spend six months in public work camps. These camps were also used to indoctrinate young men with Nazi propaganda.

Autobahns. The labour service provided the main workforce for a massive programme of road building, see Source 31. Over 7,000 kilometres of new 'autobahns' (motorways) were planned and by 1938 nearly half of them had been built. The Nazi propaganda machine projected an image of Hitler as the 'supreme worker'. He often made public appearances to set an example for his workforce, as you can see from Source 32.

▲ SOURCE 31
Celebrations in 1936 to mark the opening of a new autobahn.

methods and they turned a blind eye to the Nazi disregard for human rights and the party's military intentions. Hitler used his propaganda chief, Goebbels, to manipulate public opinion in favour of Nazi policies.

The National Labour Front
Workers in Hitler's Germany did not have trade unions to protect their rights or provide benefits. Instead the Nazi Party set up a National Labour Front under the leadership of Doctor Robert Ley. Its

programme of 'strength through joy' offered holidays for 'model workers'.

Another incentive for German workers was the introduction of an affordable car: the Volkswagen or 'people's car'. About 300,000 workers paid regular subscriptions before the Volkswagen went into production, but by the time the Second World War broke out, none of them had received a car. The factories were used to manufacture military vehicles for the war effort.

Hitler successfully fought the problems of the Depression, but many of his economic plans also served a military purpose and after 1939 the world had to face the longer term consequences of Nazi government in Germany.

▲ SOURCE 32
Hitler announces his 'battle for work' campaign as the building of one of the first autobahns gets under way in March 1933. Goebbels (wearing a Nazi armband) is standing behind Hitler.

QUESTIONS

1   *Compare Roosevelt's and Hitler's respective styles in attempting to win back public confidence after the Depression.*

2   *One feature common to both the American and German approaches was strong government action. Look ahead to how the British government coped with the Depression (page 43). What comments would you make?*

Simulation

It is 1934. You are a member of a Jewish trading family living in a German city. Since the Great Depression the business has struggled. You have heard from relatives that business is picking up in the USA as a result of the New Deal. You also have a feeling that life may become difficult for Jews in Germany under Hitler. With the family savings you could all emigrate to the USA. In groups of four, hold a family discussion to decide what you should do.

What was the impact of the Depression on the Soviet Union?

The political system in the USSR ensured that it was protected from the effects of the Depression. Yet Stalin's DICTATORSHIP meant that the price paid for this 'protection' ranked amongst the worst excesses ever carried out against humanity.

Five Year Plans

Under the last of the Tsars some industry had grown up in Russia. However the 1917 Revolution and the Civil War of 1918 to 1921 caused terrible disruption. Agriculture was still backward and primitive. This was the economic situation which Joseph Stalin faced when he became ruler of the USSR in 1928. He stated his priority for survival, see Source 33.

Attempting to move the Soviet Union so quickly required tough and total planning. Stalin made use of Gosplan, the State Planning Commission. From 1928 onwards, a series of Five Year Plans was constructed as a blueprint for a communist economy. A list of targets for key industries, energy and transport services were not just suggested but demanded. These in turn were translated into production targets for each particular factory and downwards, again, to sections of workers within factories. Source 34 indicates that mostly output failed to meet targets, but it does not mask the remarkable achievements which lay behind the increases.

Targets were one thing. To be attainable, however, a complete change of workers' attitudes was essential. Loyal workers were exhorted to ever greater efforts through a barrage of party propaganda. As a result, millions of Russian workers worked themselves to early graves to achieve the figures shown in Source 34. Women workers were needed too, and posters such as Source 35 encouraged them to work.

STAKHANOVISM, see Focus, had harmful effects on other workers, since subsequent targets were often raised to impossibly high levels. Bureaucratic bungles, incompetence and corruption also made fulfilling the demands of the State almost impossible.

SOURCE 33

We are fifty or a hundred years behind the advanced countries. We must make good this distance in ten years. Either we do it, or we shall be crushed.

(An extract from a speech Stalin gave in 1931.)

	1928 Production	1932 Target	1932 Actual Production
Electricity (M KWh)	5.1	17.3	13.6
Coal (Million tonnes)	36.0	69.0	65.3
Oil (Million tonnes)	11.9	19.3	21.7
Pig-iron (Million tonnes)	3.4	8.1	6.3
Steel (Million tonnes)	4.1	8.4	6.0

▲ SOURCE 34
The first Five Year Plan, 1928 to 1932.

Agriculture

The Five Year Plans needed new cities and new workers. The peasants would have to provide food for these cities. Stalin also wanted to export food to buy vital foreign-made equipment. So the Five Year Plan set about re-organising agriculture, too. Individual peasant holdings were abolished in a COLLECTIVISATION programme. With larger fields, modern methods using tractors and fertilisers could be introduced. The peasants were bitterly opposed to the changes introduced by the programme.

QUESTIONS

1 Draw bar charts from Source 34 to show the intended and actual production figures achieved in the first Five Year Plan.

2 Study Source 35. What impressions of the developing Soviet economy is the artist trying to show?

3 How useful is Source 36 as evidence about Stalin's Russia?

4 'Stalin's legacy is that he achieved his aim in Source 33. The proof was in the Soviet defeat of Nazi Germany, for which the Western democracies have since taken much of the credit'. What is your opinion of these statements?

◀ **SOURCE 35**
A poster commemorating the 30th anniversary of the Russian Revolution, it says 'long live our triumphant collective farm peasantry'.

1917

1947

ДА ЗДРАВСТВУЕТ НАШЕ ПОБЕДОНОСНОЕ КОЛХОЗНОЕ КРЕСТЬЯНСТВО!

Purges

Alongside targets came a system of state-organised terror on an unprecedented scale. The 'PURGES' which began in 1934 removed key political figures opposed to Stalin who would find themselves arrested, imprisoned and tried in 'show trials'. Once found guilty they were either executed or sentenced to hard labour. In addition, any dissident seen to be critical of Stalin, his politics, the Communist Party structure or local officials was likely to suffer a similar fate. Secret police and government informers made free discussion impossible and dangerous. Kulaks – better-off peasants who opposed or might oppose collectivisation – were also at risk from the purges. Thousands of Soviet prison camps were established in remote zones where 'political prisoners' spent years, without trial. They accounted for a decrease of 20 million in the Soviet Union's population.

What was Stalin's economic legacy?

By a mixture of co-operation and coercion, the Soviet Union was dragged into the 20th century, but at a terrible price in freedom and in standards of living. Average living standards for Russian families in towns and cities were no better by 1952 than they were in 1928. Because of widely differing baselines, other economic comparisons between East and West are invalid. To this day, Russia's fragile economy – in a world context – bears witness to the Stalin years.

F**O**CUS ...*Stakhanov and Solzhenitsyn*

Alexei Stakhanov achieved fame in 1935 when in one five-hour coal shift, his team dug 102 tonnes of coal (14 times above the standard target). Through propaganda, Stakhanov was made a heroic example for other 'Stakhanovites' to follow. Stakhanov was given party privileges like extra holidays and better housing.

Alexander Solzhenitsyn was a DISSIDENT writer who criticised Stalin. He was arrested in 1945 and spent eight years in prison camps. Many of his books were banned in Russia. Source 36 is an extract from a novel about life in a prison camp. Solzhenitsyn was awarded the Nobel Prize for Literature. Eventually, he left Russia for the USA where he continued to write and to campaign for the release of other imprisoned dissidents.

"

SOURCE 36

Without neglecting a single fish scale or a particle of flesh, Shukhov went on. He ate everything – the gills, the tail, the eyes when they were still in their sockets.... The cold stung... fog wrapped itself around and made them cough. The temperature out there was minus 27 degrees. The prisoners now clad in all their rags, a card around their wrists, waiting within leaden hearts for the order, 'Out you get'.

(An extract from Alexander Solzhenitsyn's novel, *One Day in the Life of Ivan Denisovich*.)

"

Unemployment in the inter-war years

How were the people of Britain affected by unemployment in the 1930s?

We have already seen, from Source 6 on page 27, that some areas were much harder hit by unemployment than others. In the Bishop Auckland area of Durham, for example, there were 33 coal pits employing 28,000 miners. By 1935, 17 pits were closed for good, and a further three were closed with a remote possibility that they might be reopened. The remaining 13 pits employed just 6,500 miners on a part-time basis. In some villages unemployment was almost 100 per cent. In West Auckland, only one man in ten had worked in the previous ten years.

The dole kept people alive but the physical hardships were obvious to all. Although people kept up the search for work, they also took up hobbies like reading, gardening, walking, carpentry or football to fill the hours. It was difficult keeping warm and occupied during the day, so many people got up late and went to bed early. Going to the cinema was another option for passing the time: unemployed young people went to the cinema at least once a week.

▼ SOURCE 37
The weekly spending of an unemployed mill-worker's family in Lancashire, 1931. Their income from the dole was £1.59.

Rent	43p
Coal	17½p
Gas	12½p
Union and insurance subscription	16p
Savings club	5p
Meat	10p
Milk	12½p
Bread	23½p
Margarine	10p
Jam	4p
Clog-irons	2½p
Total	£1.56½

SOURCE 38

Two thousand people attended in pouring rain outside the Broadway Theatre, Eccles Cross, today, to apply for 35 jobs. Two men had walked from Oldham (a distance of 12 miles) and after being interviewed were faced with another long walk home in the rain. Applicants were early. Half a dozen waited all night. Some women turned up at a quarter to six. Then the crowd began to gather in earnest. The rain drenched the overcoatless and ran in streams from umbrellas, but no one would give up his or her position.

(An extract from the *Manchester Evening News* from 15 July 1932.)

◄ SOURCE 39
This photograph of the deserted Palmer's shipyard in Jarrow was taken in 1933.

SOURCE 40

If only he had work. Just imagine what it would be like. On the whole my husband has worked about one year out of twelve and a half. His face was lovely when I married him, but now he's skin and bones. When we married he had a good job. He was earning £8 to £10 a week. He's a left-handed ship's riveter, a craft which should be earning him a lot of money. He fell out of work about four months after I was married so I've hardly known what a week's wage was.

(Oral evidence collected in 1935 by Felix Greene, from a shipbuilder's wife.)

To find out how unemployment on this scale affected people, historians have used different types of evidence: statistics, newspapers, contemporary photographs and oral evidence as well as impressions from contemporary journalists and writers, see Sources 37 to 43.

Government action

In comparison with the dynamic policies of the governments of the USA, Germany and the USSR which have been outlined on pages 38 to 41, British governments did little to tackle unemployment. The National Government which took control in 1931 was led by the Labour politician, Ramsay MacDonald, until 1935, but its policies were Conservative (see page 33). Tariffs were put on imported goods, such as iron, steel and food, to protect British industry and agriculture from foreign competition. Shipyards had been closing fast, with disastrous consequences for shipbuilding towns like Jarrow, see Source 39. Grants were given to shipping firms so they could place orders for new ships, such as the *Queen Mary*. Work was started on this ship on Clydeside in 1933, but this kind of government spending was exceptional.

The Special Areas Act of 1934 was designed to give work to unemployed people in schemes such as building roads and recreation grounds. However the scheme did not have enough money or power to be very successful in reducing unemployment. Lloyd George attacked the Act in the House of Commons, contrasting its effectiveness with the success of the New Deal in the USA. In 1937 the scheme was extended to attract firms to special trading estates in depressed areas. Firms were encouraged by the government to relocate to these estates with a package of incentives.

▲ **SOURCE 41**
A photograph of an unemployed miner from Wigan with two children, taken in 1939.

③ Target Questions

1   *Study Sources 38, 41 and 42. Which do you think is more useful for telling us about how people reacted to unemployment?*

2   *Do you think that oral evidence, like Source 40, is more or less reliable than the impressions of visiting writers like Priestley and Orwell, Sources 42 and 43?*

3   *Source 37 is accurate, but how useful is it?*

4   *Sources 40 and 42 may not be reliable; how would you use them in an enquiry into the lives of unemployed people in Britain in the 1930s?*

5   *What problems are there in finding out exactly what people's lives at that time were like?*

SOURCE 42

"There is no escape anywhere in Jarrow from its prevailing misery. One out of two shops appeared to be permanently closed. Wherever we went there were men hanging about, not scores of them, but hundreds and thousands of them."

(From a description of Jarrow written by J.B. Priestley. He visited Jarrow in 1933 and recorded his impressions in an account called *English Journey* which was published in the same year.)

SOURCE 43

A working man does not go to pieces under the strain of poverty as a middle-class person does. Take for instance the fact that the working class think nothing of getting married on the dole. It is a proof of their good sense. They realise that losing your job does not mean that you cease to be a human being.

(From *The Road to Wigan Pier*, by George Orwell. It was published in 1937.)

Why did fascism fail in Britain in the 1930s?

Today, the idea of the British political system becoming a one-party state led by a right-wing dictator seems unlikely. Yet in the 1930s it was not such an absurd possibility. Britain was in crisis. Millions of people were unemployed. The old ways of running things seemed quite unable to cope. At the same time, it seemed that Nazis, led by a charismatic dictator, were solving Germany's economic problems. And in Italy, Mussolini and his FASCIST party appeared to be improving the economic situation. Other countries in Europe were abandoning democracy in the crisis of the Depression. Could the British electorate be driven to vote for more extreme political parties offering radical solutions to the crisis? Who might come forward with the necessary charisma to be the British equivalent of Hitler or Mussolini?

There was indeed a shift towards political extremism in Britain in the 1930s. Many turned away from mainstream party politics to the Communist Party. Others joined the British Union of Fascists. You can see some of the events in the rise and fall of British fascism in the time chart.

The British Union of Fascists

Sir Oswald Mosley (Source 44) was considered a bright young Labour MP in the 1920s. When the Depression hit Britain he called for drastic action to be taken including spending money on job creation schemes. His ideas were ignored and in disgust he resigned from the Labour Party to set up his own organisation modelled on fascist parties abroad. As time went by, the public and politicians began to see the true nature of Mosley's 'party', the British Union of Fascists (BUF). It was a PARAMILITARY organisation attracting young members (known as 'blackshirts') who wore uniforms, undertook rigorous training and swore loyalty to their leader. Their meetings were often violent, characterised by tactics of intimidation and the expression of extreme nationalist and ANTI-SEMITIC views.

The BUF justified its political programme on the basis of what the 'British nation' needed. Existing problems were blamed on certain individuals or sectors of society, see Source 45. Support for the BUF was limited but its meetings and marches often resulted in violence, like the notorious Battle for Cable Street in 1936 (Source 46). Mosley's public image at these events was modelled on the behaviour of Hitler and Mussolini, see Source 47.

▼ **SOURCE 44**
Sir Oswald Mosley, a wealthy baronet, emerged in 1931 as the self-styled leader of a right-wing party which became the British Union of Fascists.

Time chart

1918–1922	Mosley is a Conservative MP.
1922–1924	Mosley becomes an Independent MP.
1925	Mosley elected as a Labour MP.
1926	Mosley becomes a cabinet minister with responsibility for unemployment.
1931	Mosley resigns from the Labour Party and forms the New Party.
1932	Mosley forms the British Union of Fascists.
1933–1934	Period of major 'blackshirt' meetings in Britain.
1936 East	Battle for Cable Street in the End of London.
1940	Mosley interned as a threat to national security.

TIME
The Weekly Newsmagazine

FIFTEEN CENTS

March 16, 1931

"BRITAIN'S HITLER"
The Bright Young People adore his panache.
(See FOREIGN NEWS)

Volume XVII

Number 11

SOURCE 46
The Battle for Cable Street, in London's East End, 11 October 1936. BUF supporters clashed with anti-fascist demonstrators and 80 people were injured.

The demise of British fascism

The Public Order Act was passed by the Government in 1937, putting an end to the activities of the BUF. Political uniforms were banned and the police were given the power to stop political marches if they feared disorder would result. As the Second World War approached, Mosley's sympathies for Hitler and Mussolini were seen as unpatriotic and a threat to national security. He was arrested after the outbreak of war and his party was dissolved.

Although Mosley had high hopes for his new party in 1931, the BUF gained very little support in the 1931 and 1935 General Elections. The victory of Stanley Baldwin's National Government in 1935 confirmed the electorate's faith in traditional politics. The British people had not turned to extremist parties to solve the social and economic problems of the 1930s. In fact, when fascist régimes in Europe began arming themselves for conflict at the end of the decade, employment opportunities in Britain actually improved as workers were taken on by munitions factories to make weapons for the fight against fascism.

SPECIAL AWARD AT THE POLITICAL ROSE SHOW.

SOURCE 45
This cartoon from 1936 attacks Mosley's dislike of Jews.

SOURCE 47
Sir Oswald Mosley leading a fascist march in 1937.

QUESTIONS

1   Why did Mosley leave the Labour Party?

2   Why did he set up the BUF?

3   Why did some people support him? What was the attraction?

4   Why did so few people support him, compared to the success of dictators elsewhere in Europe?

45

Britain in the 1930s

The people photographed in Source 48 were all on holiday at Butlin's first holiday camp in 1937. Who were these people? As we have seen from pages 43 and 44, life for people on the dole was harsh and difficult, but not everyone suffered these hardships. Areas where new industries were developing did well in the 1930s. Many of these new firms set out to build better relations between bosses and workers, as Source 49 describes.

This was not, however, the case in the new, highly successful car industry. William Morris set up his factory in Oxford in 1912 and introduced assembly line methods in the 1920s. He reduced the price of the Morris Oxford from £325 to £225, selling enough at the lower price to justify the reduction. He also brought out the Morris Minor to sell at £100. His main rival, Herbert Austin also brought out a small car, the Austin Seven. Both men ran their factories personally, hiring and firing workers as they pleased.

Average wages rose steadily, from £2-14-0 (£2.70) in 1924 to £3-11-0 (£3.55) by 1938. At the same time prices were almost stationary. Many new industries opened up assembly line jobs for women such as putting together radio parts or sewing car upholstery.

People on a steady income could afford to buy their own homes. New houses, like those in Source 50, were built on the edges of towns, often along main roads. This 'ribbon development' was the source of much criticism.

Families were now much smaller as comparison between Source 51 and Source 25 on page 18 makes clear. The birth rate fell from 24 births per 1,000 in 1920 to 16 per 1,000 in 1930. At the same time general health, particularly child

▲ **SOURCE 48**
Happy campers at Skegness, the first Butlin's holiday camp which opened in 1937.

> ### SOURCE 49
>
> They paid more wages than the local rate and more than the union rate. The men got a week's holiday and took it when they wanted it, rather than when they were told. Also they gave them an extra week's money to spend. That was considered quite something in those days.
>
> (An employee from Brunner Mond describes conditions. Brunner Mond was a German based chemical company which merged with three other companies to form ICI in 1926.)

health, improved. Between 1900 and 1940 deaths per million from measles fell from 394 to 21, for whooping cough they fell from 356 to 17, and for diphtheria from 290 to 62. With smaller, healthier families, people felt they could afford to have a better quality of life.

Time off

The most popular form of home entertainment was the radio. The British Broadcasting Corporation (BBC) began in 1922 and the number of radio licences increased from three million in 1930 to nearly nine million in 1940. The most popular programmes were 'variety shows' which broadcast a mixture of music and comedy and were a sort of radio version of the music hall (see page 23). The BBC also

Attractive FREEHOLD HOUSES **13/6** WEEKLY REPAYMENTS AT ENFIELD

From £512 £25 Deposit. Tiled kitchens and bath-rooms, gas cooker, and copper, elect. fittings, hot water system, panelled bath, garage space. NO ROAD CHARGES.

HADDON ESTATE

SUPER **1933** HOMES

BARNEHURST PARK ESTATE BARNEHURST, KENT
9/6 WEEKLY **£395** FREEHOLD
Estate Office : Station Approach, Barnehurst, Kent. Telephone : Bexleyheath 408.

NEW IDEAL HOMESTEADS LTD
BRITAIN'S BIGGEST BUILDERS

▲ **SOURCE 50**
Advertisements for new houses.

felt it had a duty to broadcast 'serious' culture, including symphony concerts, operas and plays. Many more people were able to listen to these programmes than could afford to go to live performances. Music loving families might also have a wind-up gramophone. This early version of a record player was set in a decorated wooden cabinet and played large, heavy records at 78 revolutions per minute.

Outside the home, the cinema was tremendously popular. Every week 20 million tickets were sold. Many new cinemas were opened. They were huge, grand, carpeted 'palaces' and gave people a taste of luxury for a 6d (2.5p) ticket (Source 52). Most films were American, and many Hollywood stars had a large following in Britain. Most towns also boasted a dance hall with a live band. Fashions in music and dance also followed American tastes: people enjoyed ragtime and jazz music and were eager to learn the quickstep, foxtrot and charleston.

Sport became even more popular, especially football and cricket. There was no television, so fans followed their teams by attending matches. A crowd of over 200,000 watched Bolton Wanderers beat West Ham by two goals to nil in the 1923 FA Cup Final at Wembley. People had more time to participate in sport too. Hundreds of village and works teams were formed following the introduction of a half day off on Saturdays.

As Sources 49 and 51 make clear, holidays were increasingly common. Only the wealthiest could afford to go abroad, but you could stay for a week at a small hotel in Britain for £2.00. Billy Butlin, a Canadian businessman, thought that British holiday resorts were boring and opened his first holiday camp at Skegness in 1937. He provided chalets for the holiday makers and all their meals and entertainment for £4.00 a week per person. During the first season in 1937, 10,000 people visited Butlin's at Skegness. Many of the 'campers' were middle-class, as Source 48 shows.

▲ **SOURCE 51**
A middle-class family on an outing to the sea by train.

1 Target Questions

1 *How was the way people in Britain lived in the 1930s different from their way of life in the Edwardian period? You will need to look back at unit 1 and should consider jobs, families, homes, entertainments and holidays.*

2 *What aspects of life in Britain in the 1930s would people who had grown up during Edwardian times find had changed the most? What things would they think had not changed?*

3 *Were the changes greatest in new technology, income or free time?*

4 *Look over pages 42 to 43. What were the most important changes to have happened in Britain in the years 1900 to 1940?*

SOURCE 52 ▶
The Granada cinema in Tooting, London, built to look like a Moorish palace.

▲ **SOURCE 53**
Cars and tractors ready for export at the Standard factory in Coventry, 1948. Britain was the largest exporter of cars and lorries in the world after the Second World War.

WE NEED

more imports from abroad (cotton, rubber, tea and the like) than our exports now pay for

PAID FOR BY EXPORTS $\frac{2}{3}$ ON TICK $\frac{1}{3}$

This can't go on. We must export one third more this year or get less and fare worse

We're up against it!   WE **WORK** OR **WANT**

◄ **SOURCE 54**
A poster encouraging people to work hard to produce goods for export, 1947.

SOURCE 55

There were a lot of post-war problems to clear up, of course, but I thought that we must push ahead.... It wasn't just nationalisation for nationalisation's sake, but the policy in which we believed: that fundamental things – banking, transport, fuel and power – must be taken over by the nation as a basis on which the rest of the reorganisation of the country would depend. We had to work fast. We had to re-build the export trade. There had to be control of masses of things that were forbidden to our own people at home. Shops would have lovely china, for export only. Very frustrating but you couldn't avoid it.

(Labour Prime Minister, Clement Attlee, speaking in 1961 about the problems facing him in 1945.)

1   Why did post-war Britain need rebuilding?

2   What had been the effects of the First World War on Britain?

3   What was British industry like between the wars?

4   What were the effects of the Second World War? Were all its effects bad for the country?

Rebuilding Britain 1945 to 1951

The British people had made tremendous sacrifices in the Second World War. Now they wanted to get on with building a better life. It was not going to be easy: Britain needed rebuilding.

In the words of the Labour leader, Clement Attlee, who became Prime Minister in 1945, the country was in a mess. Factories and houses were in ruins. Industry which had been geared up to the war effort now had to adjust to peacetime production. The costs of war had left Britain saddled with debts of £3,300 million. Britain had already lost some trading links as a result of the First World War and the long inter-war depression left British industry run down, old-fashioned and uncompetitive. As if these short-term and long-term problems were not enough, the new Labour government was committed to spending money on building the Welfare State, see pages 56 to 57.

However the legacy of the war years was not all bad. Wartime controls in industry had been necessary and an important cause of eventual victory. Labour was now prepared to direct the economy to deal with the problems. There were also new technologies developed in wartime, such as electronics, which could be applied to peacetime production. How did the Labour government tackle these economic problems?

Exports
Controls were put on industry, requiring goods to be made for export only, see Sources 53 to 55. With much of Europe and Japan in ruins, it was not hard to sell exports. By 1951 British exports were up 77 per cent on the 1939 figure.

Nationalisation

Another important Labour policy was to NATIONALISE key industries, by taking them out of private hands and running them as part of the government, but 'on behalf of the people' (see Source 56). The Bank of England was nationalised in 1946, the coal and electricity industries followed in 1947, the gas industry, rail transport, road and canal haulage in 1948, civil aviation and iron and steel in 1949.

Attlee justified his policy of nationalisation on purely practical grounds as Source 55 makes clear. However there were also political reasons for nationalisation: it was at the heart of socialism. Socialists had seen private enterprise failing to invest in new technology. They knew that private employers often treated the workforce badly. They looked to nationalisation to make such industries more efficient by planning and investing government money. Socialists also expected industries run 'on behalf of the people' to be better employers.

However, nationalisation did not bring about these expected changes in industry. There were some improvements in health and safety: in the coal industry deaths from mine accidents fell by 50 per cent in the first 10 years of nationalisation. But Britain was never sure how to regard its nationalised industries. Were they to be part of national planning, as Attlee suggested? Should they serve the people? Should they make a profit? We will find out more about this dilemma on page 51.

Austerity and Marshall Aid

Wartime hardships continued after 1945. Housing was in short supply (see page 57) and rationing was even tougher than it had been during the war. Then, at the end of 1946, a very harsh winter set in. Coal supplies could not meet the demand for fuel and a series of long power cuts followed. Many factories had to halt production and two million workers became unemployed.

People worked in their offices by candlelight. Lifts and traffic lights went out of action. It became illegal to use any electricity in the home between 9 am and 4 pm except for two hours at lunchtime. These harsh measures were known as 'austerity'. However, things would have been even worse but for US Marshall Aid (see page 122) as Source 57 explains. Marshall Aid paid a total of $3.1 billion to Britain between 1948 and 1952.

▲ **SOURCE 56**
The coal industry was nationalised in 1947. In all, about 20 per cent of British industry was brought under public ownership.

SOURCE 57

Rations of butter, sugar, cheese and bacon would all have had to be cut by over one third and there would have been less meat and eggs. Cotton goods would have disappeared from the shops, supplies of shoes would have been cut. Most serious of all, supplies of raw materials for industry could have been affected, bringing unemployment up to 1,500,000.

(An extract from the *Board of Trade Journal*, published in 1948. It describes what life would have been like in Britain without Marshall Aid.)

1 **What were the short-term and long-term problems facing Britain in 1945?**

2 **How had the Second World War affected Britain?**

3 **How did the policies of the Labour government differ from those of the National governments in the 1930s? (You will need to look back at page 43.)**

4 **On the basis of what you have read on these pages, how successful was the Labour government in rebuilding Britain between 1945 and 1951?**

'You've never had it so good'

From 1950 Britain began a 20-year boom. The economy grew, unemployment was low and average wages rose from £8-8-0 (£8.40) a week in 1951 to £37 a week in 1972. In 1957 Prime Minister Harold Macmillan told the people of Britain 'You've never had it so good'.

With secure jobs, good wages, smaller families and many more women working, families were able to buy more consumer goods and take holidays abroad. There were two million cars on the road in 1950 and by 1975 there were 13 million. New shopping centres (see Source 58) and supermarkets changed people's shopping habits. Other effects of the boom on people's lives are discussed in unit 4.

Growth industries included the manufacture of cars, aircraft and chemicals. At the same time there was a shift from manufacturing towards service industries, especially banking, insurance, the media, telecommunications, shops and tourism. In 1950 manufacturing and service industries both employed 42 per cent of the nation's workers; by 1980 62 per cent of workers were in the service sector while only 26 per cent were employed in manufacturing.

▼ SOURCE 58
Croydon's shopping centre, photographed in 1968.

World trade in the 1970s

The post-war boom was heavily dependent on oil for heating, transport and power. One third of the world's oil supplies came from the Arab countries of the Middle East. When the Arab attack on Israel in 1973 failed – the Yom Kippur War – Arab oil producers decided to cut back supplies to countries which supported Israel. There was an immediate energy crisis and inflation went up to 30 per cent in 1973 to 1974. Since then, energy has never been cheap, and world trade has become much more competitive.

The British disease

Britain has found it hard to compete in this stringent economic climate. Take the example of a key industry, car manufacture. In 1965 95 per cent of cars on British roads were British made, by 1980 the figure had fallen to 43 per cent. Productivity in the British car industry was low. In 1976 each British car worker made five cars, compared with eight cars for every worker in Germany and 28 in the highly automated US car industry. Many people were aware of the problem of low productivity but, as Source 59 shows, it was not tackled.

Why not? This lack of competitiveness: high prices, unreliable delivery and poor after sales service has been called the 'British disease'. But who was to blame for the poor health of British industry? Inevitably, everyone blamed everyone else.

Employers blamed the trade unions. They said unions were more interested in holding on to jobs and pushing up wages than modernising the industry by introducing new technology, see Source 60.

QUESTIONS

1   Does Britain still suffer from the 'British disease'? What do you think are the causes?

2   Does the study of Britain's history help you to understand the causes of the 'British disease'?

3   Talk to other people about this. What do they think? Try to find a range of opinions.

"I'LL ATTEND TO THE FOUNDATIONS LATER"

SOURCE 60

It was the trade unions. Their attitudes towards progress were lamentable. Simple things: a portable hand-welding machine where one man could easily work four machines and in Sweden they did, ditto in Germany, ditto in France. In Britain, one man to one machine.

(Sir Leonard Redshaw, who ran Vickers shipyards, blames the unions.)

SOURCE 61

If the men had been given better job security, sick pay, pensions, better working conditions, and that was possible in the 1960s with the vast profits they made, then in my opinion they could have won the co-operation of the workers. But they felt they had a divine right to rule and if the management attitude is of that nature then workers react in a not very positive manner.

(A Clydeside trade unionist blames the bosses.)

The unions blamed their employers. In the old industries like shipbuilding, relations between employers and employees were bad and unions were tough. The speaker in Source 61 thought the boom years could have been used to improve relations, but the old divisions remained. For example, at the British Aerospace factory there were four canteens, one for each grade of employee.

The government was blamed by everyone. Governments were not sure what their aims were. Policies of encouraging factories to move to areas of high unemployment tended to make industries less competitive. For example, in 1948 the government persuaded Ford to move to Liverpool and ICI to set up a plant in Pontypool. Both firms would have preferred to build factories in the Midlands. When the Conservatives de-nationalised the steel industry in 1953, they still influenced the location of two new plants at Llanwern in South Wales and Ravenscraig in Scotland where unemployment was very high.

Governments had to make a difficult choice: did they want industry to be more competitive or to provide a social service? It was the nationalised industries like coal and the railways that suffered the most from these confused aims. Should coal be cheap to help industries which used coal as fuel? Or should it be more expensive to generate more money to invest in the mines and make them more competitive? Governments faced a similar dilemma on the railways: should they be run to make a profit or to provide a service for the public, if necessary out of taxpayers' money? The Beeching Report in 1963 proposed that 14,500 kilometres (about 40 per cent) of the country's rail network should be closed as it was not profitable. However there was huge opposition to the report, especially from people who relied on the threatened lines. The result was, as usual, a fudge: some lines were saved, and only 9,600 kilometres closed. But was the government prepared to pay for the losses on the lines which remained open?

Equality at last?

Has there been any progress towards equal rights for women in the last 50 years? If so, has it been because of the Second World War, changes in the law or economic pressures?

Women took on even more vital jobs in the Second World War than they had in the First World War. However in both wars, it was made clear that this was meant to be a temporary situation. Even the government poster shown in Source 62 told women that their work was just needed 'for a little longer'. After 1945 women returned to the traditional roles they had played in the 1930s. For most women, the first priority was still running a home and looking after the children. If they had any kind of job, it had to fit around their family commitments. Only a few women, usually unmarried, pursued a career.

However the boom years of the 1950s and 1960s brought some changes. With more labour-saving gadgets in the home, smaller families, and the pressure to have

SOURCE 62▶
A poster from 1946 encouraging women to work.

▼ SOURCE 64
Women working on an assembly line, photographed in 1954.

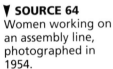

SOURCE 63

The lowest-paid sector of the workforce is made up of women. In 1976 43 per cent of full-time women workers earned less than £40 a week, compared to only 5 per cent of men. Despite the fact that women make up 40 to 50 per cent of the workforce, the proportion of women in top jobs is low.

(An extract from the Report of the Equal Opportunities Commission, published in 1978.)

money to spend, more and more women wanted to work. In 1951 22.6 million women went out to work, by 1976 this number had risen to 25.9 million. Women usually took low paid, routine jobs. You can read a description of what their work was like in Source 63 and in Source 64 you can see women working on an assembly line.

Changes in the 1970s

For women it was not the notorious 1960s which brought change, but the 1970s. Important laws were passed. The Equal Pay

Act, 1970, stated that men and women doing the same job should get the same pay. (However, some employers got round this by creating differences between jobs for men and women.) Under the terms of the Sex Discrimination Act, 1975, all jobs were to be open to women on the same basis as men. The Equal Opportunities Commission was set up to monitor equality in the workplace.

Women's movements

There are limits to how far laws can change attitudes, but nevertheless attitudes did begin to change in the 1970s. Radical movements in the 1960s (which we discuss on pages 68 to 69) paid little attention to women's equality. However the calls for freedom and equality in society as a whole led women to look at their own situation. The women's movement grew in the 1970s, giving women mutual support. It worked hard to change attitudes and improve the status of women. Women campaigned for their rights across a range of issues from jobs to politics, from abortion to the use of discriminatory language.

Another important change which brought women greater freedom was the contraceptive pill. It was first made available on the NHS in 1974, giving women control over their sex lives and allowing them to make their own decisions about motherhood. Since the 1970s many women have chosen to make a successful career and then have children when they are older.

Women at work and in politics

Between 1971 and 1986 average earnings for women went up from 64 per cent to 74 per cent of the average male salary. Women began to break into high status, well paid and male dominated professions. From 1975 to 1986 the number of women qualifying as solicitors rose from 19 per cent to 54 per cent of the total, as qualified accountants from 7 per cent to 23 per cent and as bankers from 4 per cent to 21 per cent.

Legally, women have had complete equality with men in politics since 1928, but in reality their position has been far from comparable. Parliamentary candidates are chosen by local party committees which are often reluctant to choose women. In 1945 there were 24 women MPs but in 1951 there were only 17 and in 1979 only 19. More recently the number of women MPs has increased: 41 were elected in 1987 and 00 in 1992.

QUESTIONS

1 **Did the Second World War change the position of women in Britain?**

2 **Do you think laws can change attitudes? How else do people's attitudes get changed?**

3 **Do you think the women's movement has been effective in winning greater equality for women in Britain?**

FOCUS ...*Margaret Thatcher and Diane Abbott*

Margaret Thatcher was born in 1925, the daughter of a grocer. After studying chemistry at Oxford University, she trained as a lawyer. In 1959 she was elected as the Conservative MP for Finchley. In the government of 1970 to 1974 she served as education minister. In 1979 she became Prime Minister and led the Conservative government until 1990.

▲ Margaret Thatcher, photographed in 1979 when she became Prime Minister.

Diane Abbott was born in 1953. She was educated in London and at Cambridge University. She worked in the Civil Service and for the National Council for Civil Liberties. She was a Labour councillor in Westminster from 1982 to 1986 and became the first black woman MP when she was elected for Hackney North and Stoke Newington in 1987.

▲ Diane Abbott.

The five giants

In unit 1 we saw how the Liberals began to deal with poverty. In this unit we shall question how effective their measures were in coping with the problems of the 1930s which were described in unit 2. We shall go on to see how the Second World War and the election of a Labour government in 1945 brought changes to the system of welfare. The unit ends by examining what has happened to the Welfare State since then.

▲ **SOURCE 1**
Want.

SOURCE 2 ►
Disease.

Key Questions

What are the factors that prevent people from leading a full and happy life?

How have governments tried to deal with these factors?

What changes have there been in welfare and health care?

How far was the introduction of the Welfare State a revolution?

Is the Welfare State good or bad for the country?

At the height of the Second World War the government asked Sir William Beveridge to investigate the National Insurance system in order to tidy it up. But he went further and in 1942 produced a vision of the future that caught the nation's imagination: the Beveridge Report.

He identified 'five giants' on the road to progress, see Sources 1 to 5. The first giant was want (poverty). As most poverty was caused by loss of earnings, Beveridge proposed a single system to pay all workers for any period when they were unable to work through illness, unemployment, pregnancy, looking after children or old age. Disease was the second giant: Beveridge put forward proposals for a free health service for all citizens. He argued that the third and fourth giants, ignorance and squalor, could be eliminated if improvements were made to education and housing. Finally, Beveridge called upon future governments to make plans for full employment in order to deal with idleness, which he identified as the fifth giant.

Beveridge proposed an

▲ **SOURCE 3**
Ignorance.

◄ **SOURCE 4**
Squalor.

▲ **SOURCE 5**
Idleness.

insurance scheme, not paid for from taxes (see the diagram on page 13). Everyone in work would pay contributions and, as a result, everyone would be entitled to receive benefits, no matter whether they were rich or poor. The benefit payments would not be means tested.

The report included measures to improve the position of women. Single women at work would pay the same contributions and receive the same benefits as men. Recommendations were made in the report for mothers to receive child allowances and for grants to be paid to pregnant women, widows and women staying at home to look after elderly or sick relatives. Beveridge also proposed that housewives should be eligible for sickness benefit.

Although the wartime government put off discussion of the Beveridge Report, it was immensely popular. Over 635,000 copies were sold and the contents of the report were widely debated. A survey carried out in 1943 showed that 86 per cent of people were in favour of its recommendations and only 6 per cent did not support the report's proposals.

The Beveridge Report was published just after the Battle of Alamein, which was regarded as a turning point in the war. People began to turn their minds to the future and to the prospect of getting their lives back to normal when the war came to an end. However, they did not want a return to the depression years of the 1930s. They wanted a new future and the Beveridge Report gave them something to fight for. The report was to play an important role in deciding the outcome of the 1945 General Election.

◄ **SOURCE 6**
EVACUEE children
leaving London in
1940.

Health and welfare in war and peace: 1940 to 1951

The Depression of the 1930s brought greater distress and need than the system of welfare set up by the Liberals before 1914 could cope with. Yet old attitudes remained: you had to prove you were looking for work before you could get the dole. Your benefit was also 'means tested', see page 58.

As early in the war as 1940 people's attitudes began to change. The dangers of bombing and invasion were shared by everyone. Evacuation (see Source 6) alerted many people outside urban areas to the poverty and deprivation suffered by many city children. At first, many adults were shocked by the condition of these children, but they became determined to see improvements made in child welfare. In 1941 free school milk and meals were introduced for all children, see Source 7.

The disruption of war created sudden, new welfare problems. Many women were widowed and thousands more had to look after their families while their husbands were away at war. Other families were made homeless. The rising prices during the early years of the war hit pensioners particularly hard. There was no time for the petty rules and means testing of the 1930s. Special

payments were made to the elderly and a system of home helps was established.

The spirit of the time can be seen in the reception given to the Beveridge Report when it was published in 1942 (see pages 54 to 55). The first of its proposals, for a Family Allowance, was passed by the Conservative Government which ran the country between the end of the war and the 1945 General Election. Eleanor Rathbone had been pressing for this kind of benefit for years, see Source 8. The allowance was fixed at 5/- (25p) a week for each child in the family after the first child. All mothers received tokens which they could cash. It was a universal benefit and was not means tested.

SOURCE 7
Children receiving free milk at school in 1947.

> **SOURCE 8**
>
> Eleanor's scale of justice was disturbed, the barrier to the achievement of equal pay for equal work could only be removed by the acceptance of family allowances. What struck her as the war years rolled by was the physical well-being and maternal efficiency yielded by small sums entrusted to the mother.
>
> (From a biography of Eleanor Rathbone.)

Labour was swept to power in July 1945 by voters who believed it was the party most likely to act upon the recommendations of the Beveridge Report. James Griffiths, a former Welsh miner, was Minister for National Insurance.

National Insurance Act, 1946. All working people paid a contribution which was recorded by a stamp on a card (the system was computerised in the 1970s). Everyone was entitled to benefit for any interruption of earnings, through sickness, widowhood, unemployment, pregnancy or old age. Grants were made available for maternity and funeral costs. Men were entitled to a state pension at 65 and women at 60. All these benefits were paid 'as of right' and were not means tested.

National Assistance Act, 1948. This was intended to help people who still faced financial difficulties. People applying for National Assistance did not have the earnings of other members of their families deducted from the benefit.

National Health Service Act, 1946. You can read about this on pages 60 to 61.

Housing

Some council housing was built between the wars, mainly under Addison's Act, 1919. Slum clearance schemes began in the 1930s. During the Second World War, nearly half a million homes were destroyed or made uninhabitable. As a result, there was a housing crisis in 1945.

Returning servicemen wanted to set up their own homes and there was a boom in marriages and babies. In desperation, 46,000 people moved illegally into disused army camps as squatters. To relieve the problem of homelessness as quickly as possible, 157,000 houses were put up using prefabricated sections made in factories. You can see some of these temporary 'prefabs' in Source 9.

The Minister for Health and Housing, Aneurin Bevan, called prefabs 'rabbit hutches'. He wanted high quality council housing and increased the standard size of new council homes being built, saying that 'nothing is too good for the working class'. However, there were shortages of building materials and skilled workers. Bevan created complex regulations to divert scarce resources from private construction into council house building. The Labour Party had promised 200,000 council houses in the first two years after the war, but only 140,000 were actually built.

New towns

In 1944, a Greater London Plan was drawn up by Abercrombie. It tackled London's problems of poor housing, traffic congestion, not enough open spaces and bad planning. The solution put forward was to establish a 'green belt' around the city where no building would be allowed. This would give Londoners some countryside close at hand. Beyond the green belt eight new towns were planned to take some of London's surplus population. The 1946 New Towns Act set up these eight new towns around London, together with a further six new towns in other parts of the country.

▲ **SOURCE 9**
These prefabs were put up in York in 1947.

QUESTIONS

1 *How and why did evacuation change people's attitudes to welfare?*

2 *What other changes did the war make to people's attitude towards one another?*

3 *In what ways were government actions over school milk, Family Allowances and National Insurance different from what governments did in the 1930s?*

4 *In what ways did the Labour government use its power to change the face of the country?*

How effective were the Liberal reforms?

As we have seen on page 15, Lloyd George's National Insurance Act of 1911 dealt with two causes of poverty: illness and unemployment. At the end of the First World War the scheme was extended and after 1920 National Insurance included anyone earning under £5 a week, except farm labourers, servants and teachers. By 1942 there were 20 million people in the health scheme and 14 million covered by unemployment insurance. However, a National Insurance system split into two separate schemes for health and unemployment seemed complicated. There was really only one problem: poverty caused by loss of earnings.

The original plan of 1911 was based on low, short-term unemployment at around 4 per cent. Benefits were paid for only 15 weeks. As you saw in unit 2, unemployment between the wars averaged 14 per cent, hitting 23 per cent in 1932. In some areas unemployment was as high as 70 or 80 per cent and people could be out of work for years rather than weeks.

In 1921 the government extended the period of benefit payment to 47 weeks and then to 52 weeks. Benefit, known as 'the dole', was paid at a rate of 15/- (75p) a week for a man or 12/- (60p) a week for a woman. It was hardly enough to live on, as Sources 10 and 11 testify. At the peak of the crisis in 1931, the government cut the dole by 10 per cent. Although the old poor law had been abolished in 1930, its basic principles lingered on. You had to prove you were looking for work, even though it was obvious to all that there were no jobs.

The government also brought in a 'means test'. Officials from the Public Assistance Committee investigated how much money you had. If you had savings, you had to spend these first before receiving any benefits. If you had any non-essential items at home, like a piano, they had to be sold before you could qualify for the dole. If any member of your family had a job, even a paper round, then the dole was cut by the amount of their earnings. Suspicions were raised if, for example, someone in your family was seen wearing a new coat. An official would be sent round to see if you had some extra money.

Unemployed people, who had lost their jobs through no fault of their own, bitterly resented the means test. After 1945, the government wanted to take a less begrudging attitude to benefit payment, see page 57.

SOURCE 10

Mrs J., a woman of 26, had as the neighbours said, 'gone away almost to a skeleton' through sheer starvation. Though she was nursing her baby, I found that all the food she herself had had yesterday was a cup of tea at breakfast time, and tea and two slices of bread and butter at tea time. The school dinner for the eldest child was divided with her four year old brother every day and saved them from utter starvation.

(An extract from a health visitor's case book.)

SOURCE 11 ►
Infant mortality (the number of children dying before the age of one out of every 1,000 born) for two British towns.

Infant mortality		
	1928	1933
Wigan	93	110
Oxford	38	32

◀ **SOURCE 12**
Slum housing in 1939. A women's health committee reported that only seven per cent of working-class women lived in good housing.

Welfare problems in the inter-war years

There were some major faults in the health and welfare system in the inter-war years:

- Insurance covered workers but not their families. This put women at home at a disadvantage.

- Health insurance did not cover treatment from dentists or opticians.

- The period of benefit was too short to deal with long-term unemployment.

- Bad housing, a major cause of poor health, was not dealt with (see Sources 12 and 13). Again, it was women staying at home who suffered most from unhealthy living conditions.

- Health care still cost money, so people in poverty had to think hard before calling the doctor.

▼ **SOURCE 13**
London slums in the 1930s.

2   *Target Questions*

A   *'A great social programme which laid the foundations of the future Welfare State.' C. Cross, 1963.*

B   *'These reforms hardly instituted a system of welfare which aimed to provide "from the cradle to the grave".' E. Evans, 1978.*

1   *Use page 15 and this page to write a paragraph in support of both view A and view B.*

2   *Which of these judgements on the Liberal reforms do you think is more accurate?*

3   *How far do the sources in this unit support either of these views?*

4   *Why are these views so different?*

5   *How far could both of these views be correct?*

Bevan and the National Health Service

SOURCE 14

Society becomes more wholesome, more serene and spiritually healthier if every citizen knows that... not only ourselves but all their fellows have access, when ill, to the best that medical skill can provide.

(In 1946 Bevan described the kind of health service he wanted for Britain.)

The health system which Aneurin Bevan took over at the end of the war was a mess. Although many workers were insured under the National Insurance scheme (see page 15), doctors still charged for their services. Often they practised 'Robin Hood' medicine, charging high fees to those who could pay and low fees to those could not. Nevertheless, there were still many people who did not seek medical help because they could not afford it. Dentists and opticians also charged. People who could not afford to visit an optician tested their eyesight by trying on glasses at the counter at Woolworths.

Although local authorities employed midwives and health visitors and controlled 1,771 hospitals, another 1,334 hospitals were run as charities. There was a huge variation in the provision of doctors and hospitals across the country. You can read Aneurin Bevan's criticisms of this situation in Source 15.

The Second World War

The old LAISSEZ-FAIRE attitude towards welfare, which opposed government involvement and planning, collapsed during the war. Wartime conditions forced the government to set up an emergency medical service to cope with casualties. This provided thousands of extra hospital beds and operating theatres. Government health campaigns, such as the one advertised in Source 16, were very successful. For example, DIPHTHERIA deaths fell from 3,000 in 1938 to 720 in 1945. Citizens of almost all other countries involved in the war suffered worse health by 1945, but this was not the case in Britain. During the war, British people accepted that firm government action was needed to make things happen and they were prepared for this kind of intervention to continue after 1945.

SOURCE 15

A person ought not to be financially deterred from seeking medical assistance at the earliest possible stage by the financial anxiety of doctor's bills. Our hospital organisation has grown up with no plan – it is unevenly distributed over the country. In the older industrial districts hospital facilities are inadequate. Many hospitals are too small to provide general treatment. Furthermore, I believe it is repugnant to a civilised community for hospitals to have to rely upon private charity. I have always felt a shudder of repulsion when I see nurses, who ought to be at their work, going about the streets collecting money for hospitals.

(Bevan's criticisms of health provision as it was in 1946.)

FOCUS...*Aneurin 'Nye' Bevan*

Aneurin Bevan was born in 1897, the son of Welsh miner and one of 13 children. After leaving school at 13, he started working as a miner. He was appointed as a trade union official and later became a councillor. Then, in 1929 he was elected as an MP. Bevan was a powerful speaker and a passionate socialist.

As Minister for Health and Housing between 1945 and 1950, he ensured that council houses were built to very high standards, but failed to meet the urgent demand

for housing. His real commitment was to the creation of a National Health Service, see Source 14.

QUESTIONS

1 *Read Source 14. What does Bevan mean here? Do you agree with him?*

2 *What was wrong with the old system that prevented people from feeling 'serene'?*

3 *How did the National Health Service try to bring people the serenity Bevan wanted?*

I can remember this particular day, she went to the optician's and got tested for new glasses then she went further down the road to the chiropodist, to have her feet done, then she went back to the doctor's and the doctor said he would fix her up with a hearing aid, and I remember her saying to the doctor on the way out "Well, the undertaker's on the way home, I might as well call in there".

(Alice Law describes her mother's reaction to the opening day of the NHS on 5 July 1948.)

▼ SOURCE 16
A poster issued during the Second World War encouraging immunisation against diphtheria.

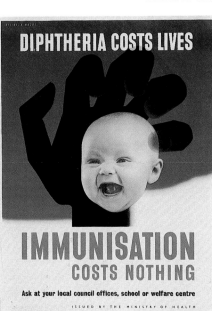

DIPHTHERIA COSTS LIVES

IMMUNISATION COSTS NOTHING

Ask at your local council offices, school or welfare centre

ISSUED BY THE MINISTRY OF HEALTH

The National Health Service

Bevan, as a socialist, believed in using the power of the government to act on behalf of the poor and the weak. As we saw in Source 14, he felt that people would not only be healthier, but would also enjoy peace of mind if they did not have to worry about getting ill. Just as his colleagues in the Labour Party were nationalising industry (you can read more about this on page 49), Bevan set about nationalising health.

Bevan's aim was to set up a free, universal service. The National Health Act of 1946, gave everyone the right to free treatment from doctors, dentists, opticians and hospitals, starting on 5 July 1948 (see Source 17). All hospitals were to be taken over by the government and their staff were to become government employees.

Doctors were opposed to this and fought hard against it. However, Bevan proved an able negotiator: he made concessions to the doctors which allowed them to keep private, fee-paying patients if they wished. As a result, 90 per cent of them agreed to enter the NHS when it started. The NHS, as one historian has pointed out, was 'the first health system in any Western society to offer free medical care to the entire population'.

The stampede

The first few days of the National Health Service were astonishing. A flood of patients sought treatment after a lifetime of suffering, see Source 18. By 1951 the National Health Service had given out 187 million prescriptions and 5.25 million pairs of glasses and dentists had treated 8.5 million patients. Critics of the NHS said that people just wanted something for nothing. Supporters replied that these statistics exposed how badly the nation's health had been neglected.

Bevan's resignation

In 1951 the government was determined to re-arm to fight the Korean War (see page 124). This meant making savings elsewhere. Within the NHS, charges were introduced for glasses and false teeth. Bevan was outraged by this breach of the principles of a totally free health service and he resigned.

▼ SOURCE 17
A patient receiving a free NHS eye-test in 1951.

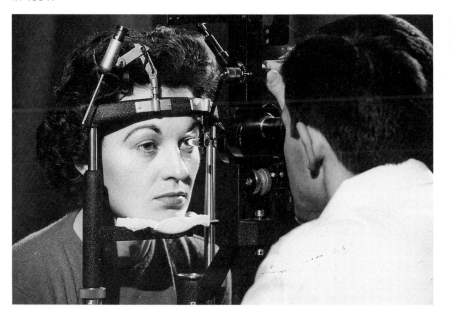

QUESTIONS

1 *The measures passed by the Labour government after the war created a 'Welfare State'. It aimed to care for people 'from the cradle to the grave'. Look back over the last four pages. How did the Welfare State look after pregnant mothers, children, workers, people who became ill, people who became unemployed, widows, and retired people?*

2 *Who do you think deserves most credit for the Welfare State, Lloyd George, Beveridge or Bevan? Discuss the contribution of each.*

Has the Welfare State been a success?

The first success of the Welfare State was to win the support of most people in Britain. Furthermore, although the Welfare State was established under a Labour government, it was supported by the Conservatives from early on, as Source 19 explains. The Conservatives were in power from 1951 to 1964 and from 1970 to 1974, yet they made no attempt to dismantle the Welfare State.

As we saw in unit 2, the 1950s and 1960s were years of prosperity. As wages increased, an unforeseen problem emerged: many working people earned far more than the levels of benefit paid by National Insurance. So people out of work from illness, temporarily unemployed or retired could see their incomes drop dramatically. Graduated pensions were introduced in

SOURCE 19

I think we should take pride that the British race has been able, shortly after the terrible period through which we have all passed together, to show the whole world that we are able to produce a social insurance scheme of this character.

(R. A. Butler speaking for the Conservative Party in Parliament in 1946.)

1961 so that people on higher incomes paid higher contributions for a larger pension. Other benefits became earnings-related in 1966 (although these were withdrawn in 1982). More and more people took out private insurance for health and old age.

The persistence of poverty

By the 1970s it seemed as if economic prosperity and the Welfare State had almost eliminated poverty. Then surveys were undertaken which showed that old age pensioners, single parents and large families living on a low wage were still in real difficulties. Four out of ten widows and pensioners were getting Supplementary Benefit (which replaced National Assistance in 1968) to bring their income up to a decent level. The number of people on Supplementary Benefit rose from 1.1 million in 1951 to 3.3 million in 1980. Another million people were probably eligible but didn't claim.

The benefits debate

The old discussion about whether or not benefits should be means tested was revived, as the table opposite shows. In 1968 health and welfare were put under the control of the Department of Health and Social Security (DHSS). Three years later, the Family Income Supplement (now called Income Support) was introduced to direct benefits to the most needy.

▲ SOURCE 20
This cartoon from *Punch* magazine presents a criticism of the Welfare State. John Bull (the British people) is being treated like a child by his old-fashioned nanny (the Welfare State).

(2) Target Questions

A 'On either side of the spectrum people are damaged. The producers in society through heavy taxation, the non-producers by being kept that way through expecting someone to take care of them.' Marilyn Daljord, 1985.

B 'It was our commitment to progress that brought in the 1940s the creation of the National Health Service and the Welfare State.' Labour Party Manifesto, 1992.

1 What are the different views of the Welfare State put forward in views A and B?

2 Which of these views do you agree with? Can you think of any evidence from this book, or from your own lives, to support your opinion?

3 Why do you think the authors of statements A and B have reached the views they hold?

The cost of health

Expectations for higher standards of health care and the growing proportion of elderly people in our population have put a greater burden on the NHS. In 1974 the NHS was reorganised, putting hospitals, their staff and General Practitioners all under the supervision of local health authorities. In the 1990s the Conservative government reorganised the NHS again, so that hospitals and General Practice surgeries would be run more like businesses, in an attempt to cut costs.

The all-party agreement over the Welfare State was broken in the 1980s. Some right-wing politicians began to criticise the whole idea of the Welfare State. They said it was ruinously expensive and that the high taxes needed to pay for free health and welfare were reducing people's incentive to show initiative and earn higher salaries. They also maintained that people dependent on the Welfare State never learned to stand on their own feet, they called it the 'nanny state' (see Source 20). Some even argued that people who have not had to take responsibility for their own welfare may lose their sense of responsibility within the community and turn to crime or violence. Conservatives who shared these attitudes believed that the Welfare State was a terrible

Views of means testing supporters	Views of means testing opponents
Means testing is better value for money as benefits can be targeted to the really needy. It is not right to pay benefits to rich people who don't need them.	All citizens should be treated equally. Means testing creates a divided society in which people feel judged.

blight on Britain (see view A in the questions opposite).

In 1973 the Child Poverty Action Group claimed that three million children were living in poverty and that poverty was increasing. The gap between rich and poor widened in the 1980s. Today, the Child Poverty Action Group has evidence that children born into poverty are ill more often, less well-educated, more frequently unemployed and have a shorter life expectancy. They have less privileged lives with fewer holidays or opportunities for leisure activities. Cutting benefits and making claiming procedures more difficult may make people take more control of their own lives, as the right-wing thinkers had hoped. But is it fair that in families where benefits have been cut, the children have had to endure hardships? Should we care about the people in Sources 21 and 22?

SOURCE 22

'I just get the kids together and say, well, I'm afraid there'll be no dinner this week.'

'How would you feel, having to rout around in a second-hand shop for three hours to find shoes for the children?'

(Poor people describe their lives, 1993.)

◄ **SOURCE 21**
A girl living in bad housing as a result of poverty, 1992.

The fifties

In this unit we will find out about popular culture in the years after the Second World War. Popular culture includes music, leisure, entertainment, religion and sport. There have been great changes in many aspects of popular culture since 1945. We shall see what these changes were and why they happened, particularly those of the 1960s.

Key Questions

What are the factors that have shaped popular culture?

How have global mass communications changed people's lives? Do we live in a 'global village'?

What were the 1960s really like?

What class and gender differences are there in British popular culture?

All the sources on these two pages are about the 1950s. For people who had suffered the Depression years of the 1930s and lived through the dangers and difficulties of the war, the 1950s came as a welcome period of relief. Rationing finally ended in 1954 and people had a little bit of money to spare. They wanted stability and were not looking for change or excitement.

In many ways, the 1950s were like the 1920s and 1930s. The radio and cinema were still the most popular forms of entertainment, although some households now had a small black and white television set. Families with cars were in a minority, but this was beginning to change. Just as they had done in earlier decades, most people who went on holiday spent one or two weeks at a British seaside resort.

Young people's lives remained relatively unchanged too: those living at home were expected to obey their parents and keep to certain routines, see Source 1. Comics like 'The Eagle' and 'Girl' were published as a deliberate effort to provide safe, wholesome reading. They were designed to counteract American 'horror comics' which were sold in Britain and considered by some 'experts' to cause violent behaviour in young people (the word 'teenager' was not used).

Middle-class men and women dressed themselves and their children in very conventional clothes, as you can see from Source 2. Women completed their outfits with hats, gloves and pearls for almost every

◀ SOURCE 2
1950s clothes for men and women.

▲ SOURCE 3
Bill Haley and the Comets rehearsing in 1957.

occasion and men were expected to wear suits and hats. Young working-class people looked to the USA for their models. They dressed more casually, wearing jeans, sloppy sweaters and checked shirts. The smarter 'teddy boy' image was modelled on clothes worn by American river-boat gamblers.

The influence of the USA was also strong in the cinema and in popular music. During the 1940s and the early years of the 1950s, popular music was provided by big bands with a lead 'vocalist'. Then in 1955, rock'n'roll arrived with the hit song 'Rock around the clock' performed by Bill Haley and the Comets (see Source 3). Elvis Presley released his first song in 1956 and quickly became an idol for young people, but his overt sex-appeal worried many parents, as the writer of Source 1 remembers.

SOURCE 1

"
Bedtime was strictly at eight o'clock sharp. I certainly wasn't allowed to stay up and watch any grown-up programmes on television.... We listened to the radio quite a bit but there wasn't much pop music on the radio then.... My parents sent me off to Sunday School despite great objections from me. Since they never went to Church I didn't see why I should go to Sunday School.... There was always a roast dinner on Sundays, followed by apple pie. It was definitely the big meal of the week.... We always had our summer holiday in Great Yarmouth.... We always stayed for two weeks in the same guest house with the same landlady.... When I was 14 [in 1960] we went to Jersey.... I was really into Elvis. He was my heart-throb and I collected all of his albums. Mum and Dad thought he was terrible and a dangerous influence, they switched off the television if he was on.

(Pat Scott describes life at home in the 1950s.)
"

Class-based culture

As unit 1 revealed, Edwardian Britain had deep class divisions. Each class had its own lifestyle, including leisure pursuits. The upper classes enjoyed a yearly cycle of social engagements. There would be visits to the country, the London 'season', lavish balls and days out at élite sporting events such as Wimbledon, Royal Ascot and the Henley Royal Regatta.

At the same time, the lower classes were developing cultural activities of their own: mass professional sport, popular newspapers and the music hall (look back at pages 22 to 23).

Popular culture

From Edwardian times onwards, these class divisions in culture have weakened, though they do still exist. Everyone watches television (although they do not all choose the same channels). People today wear similar fashions (but some clothes cost more than others). Most families have a car, go on holiday and listen to the same music. What factors have led to this increasingly widespread popular culture?

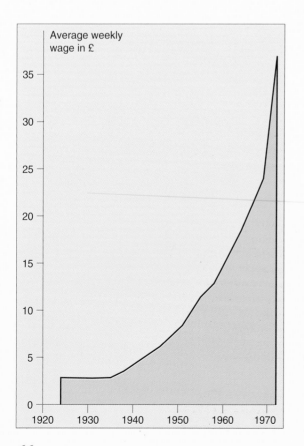

▲ SOURCE 5
The cover of *Vogue* magazine from January 1925.

◄ SOURCE 4
This graph shows the growth of average wages during the 20th century.

Average weekly wage in £

Income

In the 1920s the average weekly wage was £2, in the early 1980s it was £140 (look at Source 4). Of course prices have risen too, but ordinary people are much better off today than they were at the turn of the century. With more money to spend, they can enjoy a wider range of activities.

Mobility

Look carefully at Sources 5 and 6. The obvious similarity between the two pictures is that a car is being used for leisure. However there are also significant differences. Source 5 shows a cover from *Vogue* magazine. When this issue was published in 1925 even the modest Austin Seven cost £165, about 80 times the average weekly wage. The sports car driven by the rich young women on the *Vogue* cover would have cost much more. By the 1950s a cheap car would have cost about £380. This was less than 30 times the average weekly wage and so would have been within the grasp of ordinary families. By the 1970s cars were priced at about 18 times the average weekly

SOURCE 6
A family outing in the car. This photograph is from 1955.

THIS is the basic 4 speed
MULTI-PLAYER UNIT WITH
BUILT-IN PRE-AMPLIFIER
PICK-UP SOCKET & AUTO CHANGE
FOR ONLY 21 GNS
MANUAL CHANGE MODEL 19 GNS

SOURCE 7
An advertisement from 1961 for a portable record player.

wage and by 1980 there were 16 million cars on the road in Britain. The family car has played an important part in leisure activities, giving people greater mobility so they may choose where they spend their free time.

Time

People have more leisure time now than they did in 1900. The average working week has dropped from nearly 60 hours to 42 hours. In addition, paid holidays have become normal and there are more bank holidays during the year. As we saw on page 14, the first old age pensions were not paid until people reached the age of 70 and were not enough to live on, so most people carried on working for as long as they could. The retirement ages for men and women were lowered to 65 and 60 in 1946 (see page 57) and, with improvements in health care, people can now look forward to a longer retirement.

Technology

With more money and more time, people are prepared to pay for new leisure activities. New technology has continued to provide them. First came the cinema and the radio. These were followed by the television and the portable record player (Source 7). Cheaper cars, jumbo jets, personal stereos, home computers and satellite dishes have all influenced the way in which people spend their free time.

Gender

Divisions between the sexes (as well as between classes) have been clearly drawn in many leisure activities. In the early 20th century, many recreational pursuits were enjoyed by single-sex groups. Pubs attracted working-class men, as did professional football and cricket matches. Women from the upper classes shared interests in music, gardening and sewing while well-to-do men went hunting, shooting and fishing. Distinctions between male and female leisure activities have become increasingly blurred in recent years but still remain.

QUESTIONS

1 How have sex distinctions in leisure activities changed during the century? Start with the examples above: the pub, big sporting events and outdoor pursuits.

2 What factors have brought about these changes?

3 Is it true that we now have a popular culture in Britain which is almost the same, whatever class people belong to?

What were the sixties all about?

To millions of young people in the 1960s, the lyrics in Source 8 summed up their challenge to the older generation. The words of this song, and many others like it, spoke of a vision for a changed society. As the 1960s progressed, teenagers developed a culture based on attitudes and values which were quite different from those of their parents. There was real hostility between the generations. In the words of a song by The Who, 'I hope I die before I get old'.

The protest generation

Young people growing up in the 1960s have often been criticised as a 'selfish generation'. That judgement only reflects part of the story. It was a time when young people rejected all that their parents stood for. They wanted to be free to make their own decisions about civil rights, politics, love, sex, marriage, careers, drugs and nuclear weapons. They gave huge support

SOURCE 8

Come mothers and fathers
Throughout the land
And don't criticise
What you can't understand
Your sons and your daughters
Are beyond your command
Your old road is
Rapidly agein'
Please get out of the new one
If you can't lend a hand
For the times they are a-changin'.

(An extract from Bob Dylan's 'The times they are a-changin', 1963.)

to the Civil Rights movement in the USA and stars like Bob Dylan and Joan Baez added their voices to the cry for equality. Young people also took part in demonstrations against nuclear weapons and the arms race (see page 117), and the war in Vietnam (see page 130). The 1960s was a decade of protest against the evils of the world that the older generation had failed to eliminate.

However the new generation could also be selfish, intent on having fun and escaping from responsibility. People grew their hair long, hitch-hiked round the world, and made love without the expectation of marriage. Many exposed themselves to the dangers of drugs, following the words of the self-styled sixties philosopher Timothy Leary who told young people to 'tune in, turn on, drop out'. Others turned to the mystic experiences of eastern religions, refusing to join the 'rat-race' which they despised.

Pop music

The feelings of young people were often expressed in pop music. The poet Ted Hughes said that Elvis Presley 'turned revolt into a style'. In the 1950s a revolutionary kind of pop music – rock'n'roll – came to Britain from the USA. Singers like Elvis and Buddy Holly enjoyed huge success. Millions of teenagers bought their latest records and listened to

SOURCE 9
The album cover from The Beatles' 'Sergeant Pepper's Lonely Hearts Club Band', released in 1967.

their songs on the radio. The BBC gave only limited time to pop music so 'pirate' radio stations devoted to pop music began broadcasting. Many adults thought rock'n'roll was a bad influence but such parental disapproval just made it more exciting for young people. In 1963 the Beatles, from Liverpool, took the music industry by storm and moved the focus of pop to Britain (see Source 9). Other groups from Liverpool – 'The Searchers' and 'Gerry and the Pacemakers' – also achieved stardom. London produced some striking new bands like 'The Rolling Stones' and 'The Dave Clark Five'.

By the time the Beatles split up in 1970, the focus had shifted back to the USA where bands from the west coast were ready to take the limelight. Bands like 'The Doors' were part of a 'hippy' generation which called for a new society founded upon ideas of love and peace. Hippies were also notorious for their use of illegal drugs such as LSD and several musicians like Jimi Hendrix and Janis Joplin died as a result of drug abuse.

The decade ended with a series of outdoor pop festivals. Over 300,000 music fans gathered at Woodstock in the USA in 1969, see Source 10.

Films and fashion

Some films from the 1960s also carried social comment. 'Cathy Come Home' was about homelessness; others like 'Saturday Night and Sunday Morning' and 'Zorba the Greek' promoted the right of individuals to lead their own lives.

Young people dressed to look as different as possible from their parents. A distinctive young people's style emerged for the first time. They had money to spend and the fashion industry boomed. The King's Road and Carnaby Street in London became trend-setting centres for young people. It was here that new fashions like the mini-skirt were first seen (Source 11). Designers like Mary Quant created styles which young people wanted to wear and fashion boutiques sold out all their stock within hours of receiving new deliveries. This was one of the ironies of the 1960s. At the same time that teenagers were protesting against big business, they helped to sustain the huge profits of the music and fashion industries.

▲ SOURCE 10
The Woodstock rock festival was staged in 1969.

SOURCE 11►
Models like Twiggy, seen here on the right, set the trend for new fashions.

1 Target Questions

1 Look back to pages 64 and 65. In what ways did the 1960s seem different to the 1950s? Think about music, fashion, differences of attitude between the generations and any other aspects of life which you think changed.

2 In what ways did there seem to be little change?

3 Do you think the 1960s were an improvement on the 1950s or a deterioration? Give reasons for your answer.

▲ **SOURCE 13**
Illegitimate births in England and Wales.

▲ **SOURCE 12**
Mick Jagger of 'The Rolling Stones' giving a free concert in London's Hyde Park in 1969 which was attended by 100,000 fans.

A permissive society?

Source 12 shows 'The Rolling Stones'. Among their hits were 'Let's spend the night together' and 'I can't get no satisfaction'. From their image on and off stage and the lyrics of their songs, they became a symbol for the sexual permissiveness of what were later called the 'swinging sixties'. But were the words of their songs written simply to shock the older generation or did they reflect actual changes in people's lives?

The 1960s certainly saw some increase in personal freedom. Homosexuality and abortion were both criminal offences until 1967 when two new laws were passed. Homosexual acts between consenting adults ceased to be a crime and women were freed from the danger and expense of the 'backstreet abortion' by a new law which made it legal to terminate a pregnancy under certain circumstances.

The changing morality was reflected in other relaxations in the law. D.H. Lawrence's *Lady Chatterley's Lover* had been censored from its publication in 1928 until a new trial in 1960 removed the censorship. West End musicals like 'Hair' and 'Oh! Calcutta' could include nudity without being prosecuted.

But were the 1960s really more 'permissive' than previous decades? The contraceptive pill was not available until 1967 and then only from Family Planning Clinics. It was not available on the NHS until 1974. Look at Source 13: how far does this support the idea that the 1960s were a decade of permissiveness?

How religious are the British?
Since 1900 the Church has been in decline, as you can see from Source 14. The Anglican Church was the largest Christian DENOMINATION in 1900 and was particularly strong in rural areas. Methodist, Baptist and other Nonconformist churches attracted larger congregations in the newer industrial towns. However, all these churches have seen their congregations fall in numbers since the beginning of the century. The Church of England has maintained its traditional links with the monarchy and the state (see Source 15). But it has also broken with tradition by introducing the ORDINATION of women priests which has threatened to split the Church as Source 16 explains. The Roman Catholic Church, however, has experienced steady growth. This was partly helped by Irish immigration to industrial towns in the 19th century.

Through the 20th century, British society has become more multi-cultural so the relative importance of Christianity has decreased while other religions – Judaism, Islam, Hinduism and Sikhism – have become established.

◄ **SOURCE 15**
A royal wedding was held at St Paul's Cathedral in London, 29 July 1981.

Do these changes mean that people are less religious today than they were in the past? There is conflicting evidence. Most British people continue to mark births, marriages and deaths with a religious ceremony. With church attendance falling and greater diversity of religious beliefs, various ECUMENICAL and inter-faith initiatives have been taken. These range from practical measures like sharing premises for worship to more ambitious schemes for co-operation.

On the other hand, changes in social behaviour on Sundays have indicated a decline in the importance of Christianity in this country. In 1900 Sunday was a day of strict religious observance. Most trains didn't run and shops and theatres stayed closed. As Source 1 on page 65 tells us, things were not very different in the 1950s. Today people are more likely to visit the swimming pool or go to a DIY shop on Sundays than go to church.

SOURCE 16

By a margin of five votes, the Church of England yesterday ended 17 years of debate with a decision to ordain women priests. The result was greeted with jubilation by women campaigners and their supporters but with dismay by traditionalists and the Vatican.

(An extract from *The Times*, 12 November 1992.)

▼ SOURCE 14
Church membership of major Christian denominations in Great Britain, 1900 to 1980.

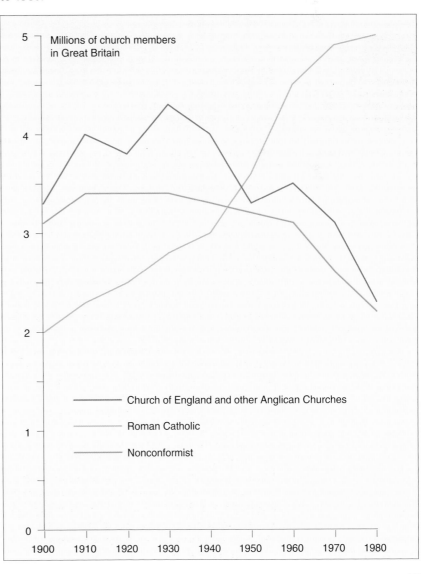

Millions of church members in Great Britain

— Church of England and other Anglican Churches

— Roman Catholic

— Nonconformist

---

① Target Questions

1 It is widely stated today that 'the permissive society' can be traced back to the 1960s. Do you agree with this view?

2 How religious are the British today?

3 How might a follower of a Christian denomination feel about either its rise or decline in the 20th century?

4 How might a follower of any Christian denomination feel about either the rise or the decline of another major faith within the area in which they live?

F**O**CUS ...*Blackpool*

By 1890 Blackpool had become Britain's most popular seaside resort. The famous tower was opened in 1894 and in 1925 the celebrated illuminations were turned on for the first time. The illuminated pier improved the nightlife of the resort and meant that the holiday season could be extended into the autumn when nights were longer. Many of the visitors to Blackpool came from the industrial areas of Lancashire, Yorkshire and central Scotland. By the late 1930s seven million people visited Blackpool each year. On August bank holiday in 1937 500,000 day trippers arrived in the town in 50,000 cars and 700 trains.

Although many people still visit Blackpool, it is no longer in its heyday and has been unable to compete with the attractions of cheap package holidays abroad.

◄ A brochure from 1932 advertising the Blackpool illuminations.

▼ **SOURCE 17**
London Underground poster from 1910.

Wish you were here

How have British holiday habits changed in this century?

Advertisements for leisure activities are everywhere: in magazines, on television or the radio and on street hoardings. We are continually tempted to travel abroad by television programmes, newspaper and magazine features, competitions offering holiday prizes or tokens to claim discounts on flights.

Until the 1960s it was only the very rich who could afford to go abroad. For most of the population, holidays were always in this country and people travelled to holiday resorts by rail (even if only for a day trip). The growth of British seaside resorts like Blackpool (see Focus), Margate, Skegness, Bournemouth, Scarborough, Southend and Eastbourne was helped enormously by cheap and quick rail travel to the coast. Some resorts, like Cromer and Ilfracombe, were actually developed by railway companies. With cheap rail travel, the working classes were able to take their holidays in the coastal towns.

As resorts grew in popularity, more hotels, boarding houses and shops opened and along the sea front there were side-shows and fun-fairs. In 1871 the introduction of Bank Holidays gave people more opportunities to get away. There were also paid 'works holidays' for employees at set times in the summer when their offices and factories closed down. Holiday camps (see page 46) were set up in many places. By the 1950s, family day trips in the car or by coach boosted the success of seaside resorts.

People living in London were encouraged to make trips to the more leafy suburbs, like Richmond, using the Underground, see Source 17. Other families enjoyed excursions into the countryside which were organised by cycling and walking clubs.

TOO MUCH OF A GOOD THING
EVERY VARIETY OF PLEASURE RESORT.
PARKS & PLAYGROUNDS
RIVER-SIDE
COUNTRY-SIDE
SEASIDE
PALACES & GARDENS.

The growth of package holidays

In the 1950s, very few British people had ever travelled overseas for pleasure. Most contact with other countries had been restricted to those stationed abroad during the Second World War. After about 1960, many British people sought alternatives to the seaside resort for their annual holiday, see Source 18. This was aided by the development of jet passenger airliners which cut down journey times and made resorts abroad far more accessible. Package holidays to coastal resorts in the Mediterranean attracted millions of British holiday makers, see Source 19. Since the 1970s, package holidays have been offered to destinations further afield, such as the USA, the Far East and Australia.

The popularity of package holidays abroad has threatened the British holiday industry. Resorts in Britain where the weather can be very changeable, have had to compete with the pull of other destinations offering guaranteed sunshine. The industry has responded by investing money in theme parks to attract day trippers. 'Center Parcs', originally started in Holland, have been particularly successful as they provide an enclosed 'weatherproof' environment for family holidays.

Despite the diminishing attraction of the British holiday resort for the 'home market', Britain is very popular with overseas tourists. In fact, tourism is an important source of income and employment for Britain.

HOLIDAYS AT HOME AND ABROAD

	Holidays in UK	Holidays abroad
1951	25	1.5
1955	25	2
1961	30	4
1965	30	5
1967	30	5

▲ **SOURCE 18**
Numbers of British people (in millions) taking holidays in the UK and in foreign resorts between 1951 and 1967.

Simulation

Blackpool or Benidorm?

It is 1967. You are 18 and live with your parents in Glasgow. Since you left school you have had a job making transistor radios and earning £12 a week. Normally you go away each year with your parents to a boarding house in Blackpool. Your parents are about to make another booking for this coming summer. But you have other plans: to go away with your boyfriend or girlfriend on a one-week package holiday to a hotel in the Spanish resort of Benidorm. Flying from Glasgow, this would cost about £60, and you have saved up enough money.

As you travel home from work, you decide that tonight is the night to tell your parents about your plans. What arguments will you use for going to Benidorm rather than Blackpool? How do you think your parents will react to your ideas? Remember to consider the differing attitudes of teenagers and their parents in the 1960s.

▲ **SOURCE 19**
A crowded Spanish beach photographed in 1966.

1 Target Questions

1 How has the pattern of holidays taken by the British changed during this century?

2 How have holiday resorts in Britain changed in the last 40 years?

Changes in mass communications

Look at Sources 20 and 21. Both show important events, one from 1953 and the other from 1969. Communications technology played a vital role in the transmission of each event to its audience. The coronation of Elizabeth II was watched by 25 million British television viewers. Without television, millions of ordinary people would have only been able to read about the ceremony, listen to a radio commentary or wait to see a cinema newsreel of the event. The coronation boosted sales of televisions which, in spite of being small and unreliable, became increasingly affordable in the 1950s and 1960s. In fact by 1965 there was a television in 85 per cent of homes in Britain.

New technology in mass communications has changed people's lifestyles. News now travels much faster, for example. In 1805 the news of Nelson's victory at Trafalgar took 15 days to reach London. Source 21 shows the American astronaut, Edwin Aldrin, on the Moon's surface. This historic event was watched by millions of people worldwide on 21 July 1969. The television pictures from the Moon were transmitted live via satellite from 380,000 kilometres away. Mass communications have made it possible for people all over the world to witness the same event at the same time.

A global village?

In the 1960s an American, Marshal McLuhan, observed what was happening. He said we lived in a 'global village'. This famous phrase suggests that when communication was slow, the village was the only size of place where everyone knew everyone else's business. Now mass communications have become so efficient that everyone in the world is able to know what is happening to everyone else. It is like living in a huge village. Do you think this is true?

At first sight the examples above seem to suggest that McLuhan was right. On television in almost every country in the world you will see some of the same commercials for the same products. Sporting events are watched by millions: it is estimated that half the male members of

▲ **SOURCE 20**
Patients and staff from a London hospital clustered around a specially provided black and white television set to watch the coronation of Queen Elizabeth II on 2 June 1953.

SOURCE 21 ▶
Edwin Aldrin walking on the surface of the Moon in 1969. Neil Armstrong and the lunar module can be seen reflected in Aldrin's helmet visor.

the human race will watch the next World Cup Final. And teenagers from Manchester to Malaysia worship the same pop idols as they watch live television coverage of concerts or pop videos, see Source 22. Television has had an enormous impact on

SOURCE 23
A cattle herder in Senegal, West Africa, listening to his radio.

SOURCE 22
Michael Jackson arriving in Thailand for a concert tour in 1993.

leisure, business, family life and politics in developed countries, like Britain. However, it is not the same in the developing world. Most people in poorer countries cannot afford to have a television set. The only time that they might be able to watch television is if they go to a bar in one of the towns or cities. Radio is still much more widespread in the developing world, see Source 23.

At the same time, some countries have resisted the pressure of big business through mass communications. Many television companies are US owned and programmes exported from the USA have contributed to the so-called Americanisation of other cultures. Fundamentalist Islamic countries object to the spread of western (especially American) values through television. Other countries have raised similar objections for nationalist reasons. By contrast, radio is much cheaper to set up and operate. Governments in many countries run their own radio stations which allows them to transmit their views and policies. Sometimes, as in Mexico for example, radio is used for educational purposes.

The 'global village' – the whole world drinking Coca-Cola and watching Michael Jackson videos – has not yet arrived.

Investigation

1 *Ask older people you know what their main evening activities were before the introduction of television. Then compare their answers with what you do in the evenings.*

2 *It is claimed that the power of television is in its ability to persuade and inform. Interview an older person to assess their reaction to this statement. Find out how they kept in touch with current affairs before the widespread availability of television.*

3 *How do you measure the spread of mass communications? Look for figures showing the numbers of telephones, televisions and radios per head for different countries. Which countries have the lowest figures? How do the figures for Britain compare with other countries? Why do these figures vary between countries? Do you think statistics about television, radio and telephone ownership provide a good indication of variations in living standards?*

Sport in the 20th century

Following sport has become an increasingly popular pastime during the 20th century. However organised sport has been changed dramatically by the influence of nationalism and the demands of commercialism.

The Olympic Games

Where are the next Olympic Games to be held? Although the Olympic Games began in Ancient Greece, they were revived by Pierre de Coubertin in 1896. Coubertin, a French nobleman, believed that an international sporting competition would foster better relations and understanding between nations, see Source 25. Today they are a good example of the influence of mass communication on sport. In the first place they are a world event – competitors take part from almost every nation. This reminds us that we are all one world. Television coverage of the Olympic Games has also brought people closer together. Millions of television viewers all over the world can now watch the same event at the same time.

Sport and nationalism

The Olympic Games have become a great nationalist spectacle. After each event, the presentation of medals is accompanied by a nationalist celebration with flags and anthems for the winning competitors. However, the Games have also been used for nationalist and political protest.

In the past, some groups have taken advantage of the media attention which is focused on the host city. For example, student demonstrations were organised in Mexico City to coincide with the 1968 Olympic Games held there. Also at the Mexico Games, two black American sprinters who won medals made a symbolic Civil Rights protest by raising black-gloved fists to the air and staring downwards as the US national anthem was played. The 1976 Games, staged in Montreal, came just after the New Zealand rugby team had gone on tour in South Africa. As a result, many black African nations withdrew their teams from the Montreal Olympics as a protest against apartheid. The 1980 Olympics were held in Moscow, only three months after the USSR had invaded Afghanistan. The USA was outraged by this action and tried to organise an international boycott of the Games. This was only partially supported but the USA, West Germany and some members of the British team did not attend. At the 1972 Munich Olympics terrorists used the occasion to kill 13 Israeli athletes as part of a continuing campaign of violence in the Arab–Israeli conflict. But the most overt display of politics took place at the 1936 Olympics held in Berlin. Hitler used the Games as a showpiece for his perverted racial ideas and Nazi propaganda. However, as Source 26 reveals, Hitler's expectations ended in disappointment.

SOURCE 25

" The important thing in the Olympic Games is not to win but to take part; just as the important thing in life is not the triumph but the struggle.

(Baron de Coubertin sums up the spirit of the Olympics.) "

▲ **SOURCE 26**
Owens won four gold medals at the Berlin Olympics. He equalled two world records and set two new ones. In the long jump, he defeated a German favourite. All this was too much for Hitler, who stormed out of the stadium and refused to congratulate any black athletes.

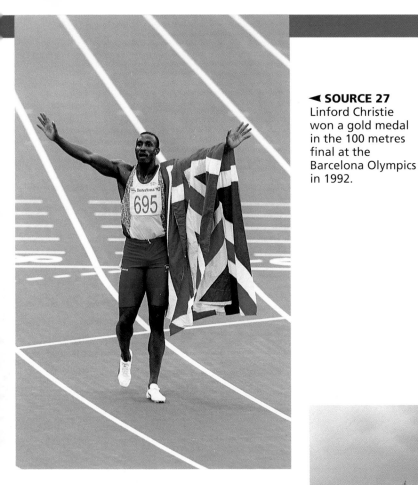

◄ **SOURCE 27**
Linford Christie won a gold medal in the 100 metres final at the Barcelona Olympics in 1992.

Think about...

1 *Today's track stars demand large 'appearance fees' to compete. How far has this practice tainted de Coubertin's Olympic ideal in Source 25?*

2 *Why do you think Jesse Owen's success in 1936 upset Hitler so much?*

3 *Has the growing commercialism of the Olympics been a reflection of 20th Century society in general?*

4 *The Olympics are criticised at times for promoting unnecessary nationalism. Explain what this means.*

Sport and commercialism

As well as nationalism, commercialism has also become an increasingly obvious feature of the Olympic Games and many other high profile sporting events. Although medallists do not win cash prizes, they are often promised long-term sponsorship contracts by manufacturers of sports clothing or equipment as a result of their Olympic achievements.

Olympic winners can also look forward to the financial rewards of being paid fees to appear at other, non-Olympic events (Source 27). Although Olympic competitors wear team kit specially designed for each country, in many other sporting events players are paid by sponsors to wear clothes which advertise a particular product. As many of these events are televised, sponsors are confident that their products will be seen by a huge potential market.

So the commercial pressures to win Olympic and other sporting events are very high. Training methods have become much tougher. The quest for achievement and prize money in sport has led some men and women to try to improve their performance by taking drugs. The Canadian sprinter, Ben Johnson, was stripped of his Olympic 100 metre title won at the 1988 Seoul Olympics after a drugs test proved positive.

▲ **SOURCE 28**
The Gateshead athletics stadium was opened in 1974. As well as being used for sporting events and rock concerts, it is also open to the public for personal fitness training.

Public participation in sport

There are healthier commercial spin-offs from sporting victories. The successes of sports men and women at an international level creates public enthusiasm and people are encouraged to join sports clubs and improve their own fitness. The Olympic achievements of athletes Brendan Foster and Steve Cram, both from the north-east, promoted a running boom in the area, see Source 28. Greater public participation in sport has been good for the leisure industry and for the manufacturers and retailers of sports clothes and equipment.

Issues of identity

In this unit we shall look at what it means to be British. How do we define Britain's national identity? We shall see how relations between the separate nations of England, Ireland, Scotland and Wales have changed during the 20th century. We shall look, in particular, at Anglo-Irish relations.

National identity is not a simple matter of places. Equally important are factors such as culture, traditions, attitudes and points of view.

The last part of the unit will study the multi-cultural nature of British society in the last 40 years.

Key Questions

How united has Britain been during this century?

Britain is traditionally regarded as a tolerant society. Has this in fact been the case this century?

What are the problems and successes of a multi-cultural society in Britain

How far has racial harmony been achieved?

Which country do you feel most closely linked to? Is it the country of your birth? The country in which you live? Or the country with which your parents identify most closely?

What images come into mind when you think of Britain? The Union Jack? Important annual events, like Source 1 at which patriotic songs are sung? Do you think of sports which you enjoy playing or watching? In some, like football, the constituent nations of Britain: England, Ireland, Scotland and Wales, field separate international teams. In others, like athletics, the British team, shown in Source 2, is drawn from all four nations.

Your own images of Britain are part of what gives it a national identity. Much of this depends on where you live.

'The Cricket Test'
British society is made up of many races and cultures. At different times there have been

◄ SOURCE 1
The annual 'Last Night of the Proms', held in the Royal Albert Hall, 1990.

▲ SOURCE 2
One example of national pride. Athletes from England and Scotland, black and white, combined to win gold in the 4 x 400m relay at the World Championships in Tokyo, 1991.

SOURCE 3

In spite of my years of residence in Britain, any service I may have given the community in war or peace, any contribution I might make or wish to make, or any feeling of belonging I might have towards Britain and the British, I ... am considered an immigrant. This term indicates that we have got into Britain ... we have no real hope of ever enjoying the desired change to full responsible citizenship.

(E.R. Braithwaite, distinguished West Indian teacher and writer, who first came to Britain in the Second World War to join the RAF, writing in 1967.)

major population shifts in Britain. People moved from rural areas to cities during the Industrial Revolution. Many emigrated, while others were IMMIGRANTS to this country. These movements have continued this century.

Migration patterns have made the concept of national identity difficult to define. In recent years Norman Tebbit, a Conservative MP, raised such problems in using 'the Cricket Test': in other words, which cricket team would Asian and Afro-Caribbean citizens support when England played against India, Pakistan or the West Indies?

Certainly, such a question raised difficult issues of personal loyalties and family history. The question also raised racial tensions, echoed in Source 3, and showed that there were very different views of what a multi-cultural society was.

2000 years of migration

1st to 4th century AD
Romans

5th to 10th century AD
Anglo-Saxons

9th and 10th century
Vikings

11th century
Normans

14th to 17th century
Dutch, Flemish
(from Holland and Belgium)

17th century
Huguenots
(from France)

18th century
Africans

19th century
Irish

Early 20th century
Jews

Mid-20th century
German Jews

1960s to 1970s
West Indians

1970s
Asians

The British people

Britain's population has grown steadily throughout the 20th century from the 32 million recorded in 1901. Results from the 1991 census suggest, however, that there may be an overall decline in total numbers: from 54.15 million in 1981 to 53.93 million in 1991.

The inhabitants of the British Isles have always been in a constant state of change because of continuous movement of peoples (see the time chart on the left). As well as 40,000 years of immigration, there has always been emigration. In modern times some 25,000 people leave Britain as emigrants each year.

Is Britain a tolerant society?
Migration has often been a last resort for people wanting to escape from economic, political or religious problems in their homeland. One characteristic of British society, noted by historians and social scientists, has been its tolerance towards new arrivals. Sometimes this in itself has acted as a major attraction to immigrants.

Views for ...
This claim of tolerance is certainly an issue which has caused intense debate among those holding widely different points of view. Many immigrant groups regard the British peoples' political and religious open-mindedness as very important qualities of its civilised society. As the Focus below reveals, many Jewish families migrated to Britain from Russia and Eastern

SOURCE 4

"The Jews of Gateshead between the two World Wars enjoyed a Judaism that was free from labels and ... political interferences. ... we were grateful to England. We were proud of our Englishness ... yet there was no need to sacrifice our Judaism in order to become more English.

Though our Jewish roots were fixed historically in ancient Israel, our patriotism was wholeheartedly for the country which had given us a home, and we fought for this country in two World Wars with the same courage and spirit as our non-Jewish neighbours.

(From *They Docked At Newcastle And Wound Up In Gateshead* by Millie Donbrow.)"

▲ **SOURCE 5**
The Jewish community in Gateshead today.

F●CUS ... *The Freed family*

- A family of Orthodox Jews.
- Originally from Minsk in Russia.
- Moishe David Freed fled to escape the POGROMS against the Jews.
- Early in the 20th century the Freed family settled among the small Jewish community within Gateshead on Tyneside.

- The father worked as a teacher of Jewish boys. Other immigrants set up businesses as tailors, picture-framers or merchants.
- As time went by a daughter of the family, Millie Donbrow, wrote down her experiences of growing up in the Gateshead Jewish community (see Source 4).

Europe to escape political and religious persecution at the hands of the Tsars or Hitler's Nazis. Upon their arrival they looked for a new life in a tolerant and democratic society. Source 5 shows the continuing Jewish presence as a distinct community within Gateshead.

Views against ...

Other residents living in Britain, notably those from non-white or non-English backgrounds, have different opinions on this same issue. To them, British tolerance can be translated as 'English arrogance'. Nowhere have feelings run higher than between the British government and Irish nationalists. Since 1969 there have been more than 3,000 politically motivated killings in Northern Ireland.

QUESTIONS

1 **What were the main reasons for Orthodox Jews to establish a community in Gateshead?**

2 **Is Britain a tolerant society? What do the arguments presented by the Freed family and Source 4 suggest?**

   Study the cartoon, Source 6.

3 **How might an Ulster Unionist view this cartoon as showing British commitment towards maintaining the majority view?**

4 **How might a Catholic Nationalist interpret the same image?**

"How marvellous it would be if they DID knock each other insensible!"

◀ **SOURCE 6**
Cartoon from the *Daily Express*, 1970.

NORTHERN IRELAND TODAY

Catholic Nationalists

One-third of the Northern Irish population are Catholic. Most believe that all Ireland and its people should be separate from Britain and a united republic. They want to see the removal of British security forces from Northern Ireland. Some pursue peaceful tactics, some do not. The peaceful political party is the Social Democratic and Labour Party (SDLP). The violent wing is the Provisional Irish Republican Army (IRA), allied to the political party Sinn Fein.

Ulster Unionists

Two-thirds of people in Northern Ireland are Protestants. Most wish Northern Ireland to remain as part of the United Kingdom with England, Scotland and Wales (hence 'Unionists'). Some are willing to fight to stay British (hence 'Loyalists'). The political parties are the Official Unionist Party and the Democratic Unionist Party. Their paramilitary organisations are the Ulster Freedom Fighters (UFF) and the Ulster Volunteer Force (UVF).

Security forces

In 1921 Northern Ireland gained its own parliament (see time chart), but since 1972 it has been ruled direct from Westminister. A mixture of police and British troops keep law and order. The Royal Ulster Constabulary (RUC) are the mostly Protestant police. Since 1969 there have been regular British Army troops in Northern Ireland.

Time chart

ANGLO-IRISH RELATIONS

1912 Irish Home Rule Bill introduced into Parliament. Unionists arm to resist it.

1916 Easter Rising

1918 Sinn Fein MPs refuse to attend Westminister Parliament.

1921 Anglo-Irish Treaty splits Ireland and gives independence to the Irish Free State, while Britain retains control of six of the counties of Ulster.

1926 Eamon de Valera founds Fianna Fáil party.

1932 Fianna Fáil wins general election in Irish Free State.

1937 In a new constitution the Irish Free State becomes known as Eire.

1939 The Second World War. Eire remains neutral.

1949 Republic of Ireland created from Eire. Total independence from Britain.

1968 Civil Rights marches in Northern Ireland.

1969 British troops arrive in Northern Ireland.

1972 Direct rule of Northern Ireland from London. Ulster Parliament suspended.

The Easter Rising

The 'Irish question' was a major issue in British politics in the early 20th century. Britain, and in particular England, has had a long and painful relationship with Ireland. During the last part of the 19th century, Irish nationalists attempted to win support in Parliament in Westminster for 'Home Rule', or control over their own internal affairs. Two Home Rule Bills in 1886 and 1893 failed to win enough support in Parliament. A Third Home Rule Bill, introduced in 1912, was under discussion when the First World War broke out in 1914. Unionists in Ulster, who feared domination by the largely Catholic South, began arming themselves in order to resist Home Rule. At the same time, extreme nationalists felt that parliamentary support for Home Rule was not enough, and looked to violence to gain their goal of freeing Ireland from British rule. There was the real threat of civil war.

A key moment occurred in April 1916. With Britain involved in the carnage of trench warfare, a group of extreme nationalists, the Irish Citizen Army, attempted to seize power in Dublin and proclaimed an independent republic led by a provisional government. The uprising was ruthlessly put down by the British Army. The rebel leaders were imprisoned and executed.

The use of history

The treatment of the leaders of the Easter Rising created so-called 'martyrs' for the republican cause. The Easter Rising is a good example of where past events in history are sometimes given an added importance, often to suit the purposes of political, cultural or religious groups today.

Nowhere in Britain are such anniversaries of past events remembered so strongly as in Northern Ireland. Many within the Catholic and Protestant communities use these annual events to glorify their 'victories' and show their 'superiority' over the other community. Often these 'celebrations' take the form of marches, parades or political rallies, with uniforms and banners. For example, while the Easter Rising may be an anniversary for the Catholic nationalist community, Protestants remember the victory of William of Orange over the Catholic James II in 1690 at the Battle of the Boyne.

1 *Target Questions*

1 *Which causes of the Easter Rising had been present for a long time and which only arose at that time?*

2 *The rebel leader James Connolly said, 'We are going out to be slaughtered'. If he felt the Easter Rising was bound to fail, why did its leaders press ahead with their plans?*

3 *Which British action in 1916 was most significant in losing the Irish people's support? Explain your choice.*
   a Intercepting German arms intended for the rebels.
   b Bombarding buildings in Dublin used by the rebels.
   c Executing rebel leaders after their arrest.

Investigation

Instructions

1 Form groups of four. Read through the information about the Easter Rising on this page.

2 Go to a new group, according to the number you are given. You are to study the source with the same number very closely. As you look at it, see if it offers any evidence about the events outlined in the Copymaster. Discuss your thoughts and record them on the Copymaster. You have a fixed amount of time for this task. Also decide how you will report your main findings to your other group later.

3 Return to your original group. You are now the only expert on your particular source. Other group members will have studied the other sources in a similar way. Decide on a logical way for each person to feed back findings (such as filling in a time chart).

4 Based on your discoveries about each source, each group should organise a brief presentation (2 to 3 minutes). It should cover the summary points on the Copymaster.

5 Following this, attempt the target questions.

◄ SOURCE 7
Liberty Hall, Dublin, 1914.
Headquarters of the Irish
Citizen Army.

▲ SOURCE 8
An artist's impression
of the scene inside the
rebel headquarters,
the General Post
Office, Dublin,
towards the end of
Easter week, 1916.

◄ SOURCE 9
Head office of the Irish
Transport and General
Workers' Union.

▼ SOURCE 11
The rebels'
surrender note, 29
April 1916.

SOURCE 10

You are letting loose a river of blood ... between two
races who, after 300 years of hatred and strife, we had
nearly succeeded in bringing together ... the great bulk
of the population were not favourable to the
insurrection (rising) ... They got no popular support
whatever. What is happening is that thousands of
people in Dublin, who ten days ago were bitterly
opposed to the whole of the Sinn Fein movement, and
to the rebellion, are now becoming infuriated against
the Government on account of these executions, and, as
I am informed by letters received this morning, that
feeling is spreading throughout the country in a most
dangerous degree...

(John Dillon, a Home Rule party MP.)

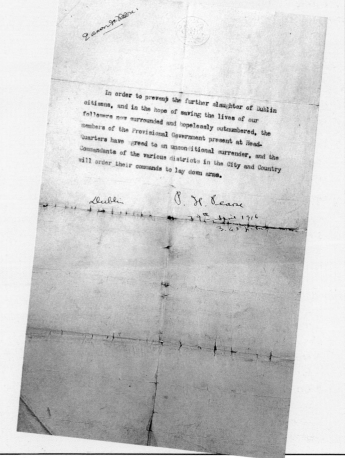

Ireland: 1916 to the 1960s

Why was Ireland divided in 1921?

As Source 12 shows, the suppression of Irish nationalism in 1916 was far from the end of 'the Irish problem'. After 1916, nationalist feeling spread across Ireland. Often this was in direct response to insensitive actions by the British authorities (see fact box below).

Sinn Fein

As a reaction to such treatment, the nationalist party, Sinn Fein, produced a policy which united all the groups who didn't think Home Rule went far enough. Its aim was to create an Irish Republic. This meant a boycott of all things British, including sending any elected candidates to Parliament in Westminster.

SOURCE 12

We seem to have lost, but we have not lost. To refuse to fight would have been to lose, to fight is to win, we have kept faith with the past and handed a tradition to the future ... If our deed has not been sufficient to win freedom, then our children will win it by a better deed.

(Patrick Pearse, a rebel leader in the Easter Rising, at his court martial, 2 May 1916.)

The result of the 1918 general election in Ireland was an overwhelming victory for Sinn Fein. True to their word, the 69 Sinn Fein MPs refused to attend Parliament at Westminster. Instead, in January 1919, many met in Dublin and declared themselves to be the elected assembly of the Irish people (see Source 13). A key figure in the election, and for much of Irish history in the 20th century, was Eamon de Valera, Sinn Fein's leader.

The Anglo-Irish War

A small group of nationalists had always favoured using violence to achieve their ends, but now the nationalists started organising their own army: the Irish Republican Army (IRA). Soon a state of war existed between the IRA and a mixture of police and ex-army recruits from England known as 'the Black and Tans'. The IRA were difficult opponents, despite their small numbers, as they used guerrilla tactics, often in remote countryside and in civilian clothing. The Black and Tans, for their part, replied with terror tactics which outraged many people.

SOURCE 13

Whereas the Irish people is by right a free people:

... for 700 years the Irish people has ... protested in arms against foreign ... takeover.

English rule in this country is, and always has been, based on force...

... the Irish Republic was proclaimed on Easter Monday 1916 by the Irish Republican Army, acting on behalf of the Irish people:

... the Irish electorate has in the general election of December 1918, seized the first occasion to declare by an overwhelming majority its firm allegiance to the Irish Republic.

Now we ... confirm the establishment of the Irish Republic...

... We solemnly declare foreign government in Ireland to be an invasion of our national right which we will never tolerate, and we demand the evacuation of our country by the English garrison.

(Extracts from the Irish Declaration of Independence, January 1919.)

BRITISH ACTIONS IN IRELAND

James Connolly, a leader in the Easter Rising, already wounded and imprisoned, was executed.

Thomas Ashe, a leading member of Sinn Fein, died after being force-fed while on hunger strike in prison.

Conscription into the British Army was to be extended to Ireland in April 1918 – although it was opposed by Sinn Fein.

THE IRISH FREE STATE

- Self-government.
- Own parliament.
- Free to make its own laws.
- To remain part of the British empire.
- MPs to swear loyalty to the king.
- Britain to remove army but to retain naval bases.
- Northern Ireland Parliament – six counties allowed to remain in the UK and not be part of the Irish Free State.

Partition

With this high level of violence, the British government was forced into looking for a solution that would satisfy both Protestant Unionists who wished to remain part of the UK, and Catholic Nationalists who wanted full independence.

The Government of Ireland Act of 1920 partitioned (split) Ireland into two states. Six of the counties of Ulster, with a mostly Protestant population, became Northern Ireland. This was given limited Home Rule with a separate parliament in Belfast, but remained tied to Britain, as the majority of the population wished. In Southern Ireland it was recommended that the remaining 26 counties should form a separate parliament in Dublin.

While the people of Northern Ireland accepted the plan and elected mostly Unionist MPs, the idea of a Dublin parliament and elections for Southern Ireland was not approved. The Anglo-Irish war broke out again. Over 1,300 lives were lost before a truce was agreed. Once again, British and Irish politicians had lengthy talks to resolve the conflicting demands. The Irish nationalists wanted a totally independent republic covering the whole of Ireland. The British government, by contrast, was only willing to grant a limited form of independence within the British Empire, and with guarantees that the Ulster Unionists would not to be forced into being governed by Dublin.

The Irish Free State

The result of the talks was the Anglo-Irish Treaty of 1921 which created the Irish Free State (see information box opposite).

The Treaty was accepted by the assembly in Dublin after a very close vote. De Valera refused to approve the Treaty and resigned from Sinn Fein. Supporters and opponents of the Treaty now split into two rival 'armies': the Free State Army and the irregular IRA. Between 1922 and 1923 a bitter civil war raged which cost 4,000 lives. Eventually the IRA surrendered their arms, but not their intentions, for a republic for all Ireland.

Eire and the Republic of Ireland

De Valera returned to power as prime minister in 1932. A new constitution was passed in 1937, renaming the Free State

SOURCE 15

Article 2 ' ... the national territory consists of the whole island of Ireland'.

Article 41.1 recognised 'the special position' of the Roman Catholic Church.

(Extracts from the Constitution of Eire, 1937.)

Eire, with two articles of great importance for later Irish history (see Source 15). In 1949, Ireland broke the final link with Britain by becoming a republic.

Since 1921 there have been certain trends in Irish history. Firstly, the Unionists took control of Northern Ireland. Secondly, economic growth was greater in Northern Ireland than the poorer South. Thirdly, the Protestant treatment of the Catholic minority within Northern Ireland created resentment (see pages 86 to 87). The IRA, declared illegal in 1936, has continued to fight for a united republic of Ireland. The Unionists, for their part, have been determined to resist any moves towards a united Ireland.

▲ **SOURCE 14**
A cartoonist's view of Partition, 1920: *The Kindest Cut of All:*
Welsh Wizard:
'I now proceed to cut this map into two parts and place them in the hat. After a suitable interval they will be found to have come together of their own accord. (Aside) At least let's hope so; I've never done this trick before.'

QUESTIONS

1 *Why did the reactions of Britain immediately after 1916 further inflame a tense situation?*

2 *Study Source 13. Which key issue did the declaration of the Irish Republic hang upon?*

3 *Explain why the IRA were, and still are, difficult opponents for the British authorities to combat.*

4 *What point about the partition of Ireland is the cartoonist in Source 14 making?*

5 *Which aspects of the Treaty creating the Irish Free State as shown in the information box on page 84 would you expect nationalists to object to?*

6 *Why might the Ulster Protestant community view the Articles of the Irish Republic's Constitution (Source 15) with suspicion?*

Northern Ireland since 1964

Why did conflict return to Northern Ireland in 1964?

Have you been personally involved in any security incidents, perhaps bomb alerts or bag searches, which can be traced back to the situation in Northern Ireland? On mainland Britain a long sequence of violent incidents such as that shown in Source 16 have taken place over the last 20 years. The violence is the IRA's way of bringing home to people in mainland Britain that the British army has been responsible for law and order in Northern Ireland since 1969. To the IRA the army is a British 'army of occupation'. There have been over 3,000 politically motivated killings in Northern Ireland since the present 'Troubles' began.

Catholic grievances

We have seen that the Protestant majority in Northern Ireland is prepared to fight to continue to be in the United Kingdom (see page 81). The Roman Catholic minority feels a closer relationship with the Irish Republic (see page 81).

To the outsider, there is little or no difference between Catholics and Protestants in terms of daily way of life. Religion and history are the key factors. Religious leaders have great influence in their communities. Sources 17 and 18 show some of the emotive language that has been used. Virtually all children go to either Catholic or Protestant schools and grow up in separate areas. Bonds of history bind the separate communities together, as was explained on page 82.

By the mid-1960s a pattern of Protestant dominance over the Catholic minority in Northern Ireland was well established. The Catholic community were victims of clear discrimination in jobs and housing. Unemployment among Catholics in 1971 was 17 per cent, compared with 7 per cent for Protestants. Local elections were weighted in favour of Protestant councillors. Londonderry, for example, has a majority of Catholics, but electoral districts were arranged so as to give Protestants a majority on the council. This meant Protestants had more council jobs and more council homes.

SOURCE 16 ►
April 1993, an IRA bomb explodes in the City of London causing massive damage.

SOURCE 17

Our glorious Reformation Heritage must be protected and Ulster must be saved from the slavery of a Roman Catholic Republic.

(Declaration of the Ulster Protestant Action Group, 1956.)

SOURCE 18

" If you allow your children to be contaminated by those who are not Catholic, then you can expect nothing but disaster.

(Bishop Farren, Catholic Bishop of Derry, 1951.) "

Discussion

Our images of Northern Ireland and its problems come mostly from the media. News cameramen, like those in Source 19, have often taken risks to obtain good footage of events. For many years, the IRA manipulated events to gain publicity for their cause. In recent years the government decided to deny the IRA the 'oxygen of publicity'. Under the Prevention of Terrorism Act prominent nationalists may be filmed speaking, but their words are not allowed to be broadcast.

What are the advantages and disadvantages of preventing Sinn Fein and IRA leaders time on TV to explain their position?

Does the media reporting of Northern Ireland events encourage terrorism?

Monitor news coverage of events in Northern Ireland on TV, radio and the press. Do you think the reports provide a balanced view?

Many Catholics also felt that the mostly Protestant RUC was far from impartial. As a result, many Catholics felt deprived of full civil rights. Even so, there was little opposition to these policies and the IRA had few supporters.

1968: a turning point

The year 1968 was a turning point in events. In the USA, the black civil rights movements reached a peak of activity (see page 93). There were student protests in France and Czechoslovakia. Their example spread to Northern Ireland where a Civil Rights Association was formed, intent on voicing Catholic grievances and demanding equal rights.

The spectre of Catholics on the march awakened old Protestant fears. Civil Rights marches in 1968 and 1969 were attacked by Protestants. As disorder grew, the RUC often failed to protect the Catholics.

Troops in

In this situation the IRA gained supporters and began to attack police stations. As a result, in August 1969, the British Army was sent into Northern Ireland to keep order. They were welcomed by the Catholics at first as more impartial than the RUC.

This goodwill did not last. IRA violence prompted the British government and Army to introduce a 'get-tough policy' in 1971. Suspected gunmen were snatched from their homes and 'interned' in high-security prison cells. All of those interned were Catholics. The policy provoked a wave of resentment and killings. Catholic support for the IRA soared and their attitude against the government and Army hardened. Relations worsened in 1972 when, in protest against internment, a Catholic march in Londonderry ended with the British Army killing 13 unarmed civilians, an event known as 'Bloody Sunday'.

Direct rule

In reaction to the escalating tension, the British government decided to take over direct control of the government of Northern Ireland in 1972.

Since then, despite attempts by various governments to create power sharing agreements between Catholics and Protestants, neither side has really been able to make it work. Too many politicians have made their names by playing on fears and prejudices to want to lose their power now. A permanent solution seems as far away as ever.

▼ **SOURCE 19**
Street disturbances between Catholic youths and British troops in the Bogside, Londonderry, February 1972.

1 Target Questions

1 Choose three of the following reasons for the outbreak of violence in Northern Ireland in 1968. Explain and compare them, showing which you think is the most important.

- Religious differences
- Historical quarrels
- Discrimination in housing
- Discrimination in jobs
- Discrimination in politics
- Violent hatred
- Irish or British nationalism

2 What have been the consequences of sending British troops into Northern Ireland and ruling the province direct from London? In the short term? In the long term?

3 Why were troops sent in? Has this decision improved the situation? Explain your answer.

Nationalism in Wales and Scotland

How have relations between England and Wales and Scotland` changed during this century?

Source 20 shows a scene before a Home Nations Rugby Union Championship match between Scotland and Wales at Edinburgh. Such events serve to remind us that as well as England and Northern Ireland, the United Kingdom is also made up of Scotland and Wales.

Indeed rugby union is one of the few sports where the various national teams contribute players to a British team for overseas tours. Source 21 shows the make-up of the one picked for the tour to New Zealand in 1993.

Sporting contests are one way in which national rivalry may be expressed. Deeper feelings may, however, lie beneath the desire for national sporting success. Political and economic decisions affecting Scotland and Wales are made by politicians in England who may have little affinity with these areas, and who may represent political parties and views with no great measure of support in Scotland and Wales. England has a much bigger population than Scotland or Wales, but does that give it the right to dominate the other countries?

How different are Scotland and Wales?
The pressure in Ireland for home rule, demanding a parliament responsible for internal affairs separate from the British parliament, was not lost on public feeling in either Scotland or Wales. Both countries had been forced into political union with England centuries before: Wales in 1536 and Scotland in 1707.

Nevertheless, Scotland has its own legal and education systems and its own church. Wales has its own distinctive social and cultural activities such as the National Eisteddfod.

The survival and maintenance of the language of each nation has been regarded as especially important. In the early 20th century Welsh was banned in schools and looked like dying out. If this happened, all the great literature in Welsh, which helps to make Welsh culture distinctive, would die

▲ **SOURCE 20**
Nationalist pride: Scotland supporters.

SOURCE 21 ►
The British Lions rugby union squad for their summer tour to New Zealand, 1993.

Squad of 30 players from which the teams of 15 would be chosen	
England	16 players
Scotland	7 players
Wales	5 players
Ireland	2 players

▲ **SOURCE 22**
A Welsh nationalist defaces a road sign in English with its Welsh version, 1970.

GWRTHDARO'R PWERAU MAWRION WEDI 1945

PETER FISHER
Golygydd Cyfredinol: JON NICHOL
Cyfieithiad Cymraeg: ERYL OWAIN

▲ **SOURCE 23**
A GCSE history textbook in Welsh.

too. The Welsh nationalists therefore concentrated on the language (Source 22). The Welsh Language Society, formed in 1962, aroused enthusiasm among the young in its campaign to protect Welsh. Today there is a TV channel in Welsh, SC4, and official documents in Wales are produced in both Welsh and English. The distinctiveness of Welsh history and society within a British context is recognised by the National Curriculum (see Source 23).

Economic differences

The separateness of Scotland and Wales was fuelled in part during the 20th century by fluctuations in the economies of the two nations. Both countries, well-endowed with natural resources, established heavy industries during the 19th century. As these natural resources diminished, industrial decline created severe hardship and high unemployment. Both areas felt resentment as south-east England prospered. Special Areas were set up to help (see page 43).

In the past 30 years, Scotland has been well placed to benefit from the discovery of oil in the North Sea in 1969. In addition, several high-tech industries have located themselves in Scotland. Pressure from nationalists in both Scotland and Wales has ensured that some care is taken by London-based governments to help these areas.

Religious differences

The religious traditions within each country have created their own tensions. In Wales, the strength of nonconformity (especially of the Baptists and Methodists) made the formal position of the Anglican Church a major issue in Welsh politics. Eventually, the Church in Wales was DISESTABLISHED in 1920.

The issue of independence

Partly as a result of all these differences, people have questioned the political relationship with England. Would independence, or some form of devolved power, in other words limited home rule, be reasonable?

Two nationalist organisations have worked towards this since the 1920s and 1930s: Plaid Cymru in Wales and the Scottish Nationalist Party (SNP). Of the two, the SNP has been more successful in converting its message into MPs. By the 1960s and 1970s, the waves of change sweeping Britain, especially among the young, found expression in spectacular by-election results for both parties. In the general election of 1974, the SNP won 11 parliamentary seats. In return for supporting James Callaghan's Labour Government, the Scottish Nationalist MPs demanded a popular REFERENDUM on the issue of home rule. Source 24 shows its outcome. Since then, the building set aside as the site for a Scottish Assembly in Edinburgh has remained closed.

The demands from the people of Scotland and Wales for a greater say in their own affairs, whether from devolution or independence, has not gone away. Many now see more powers being given to the regions through the European Community (see page 109) in the same way as other regions in Europe such as the Basque country or Catalonia in Spain.

Talking Point

Do you think Wales and Scotland should be allowed to separate from the United Kingdom if they want to?

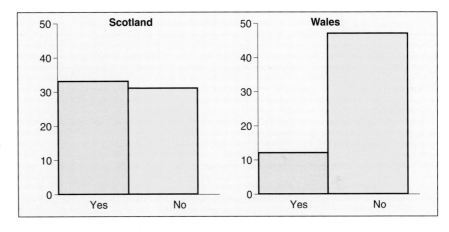

▲ **SOURCE 24**
The results of the referenda on devolution for Scotland and Wales held in January 1979. A minimum of 40 per cent of all voters had to vote yes for the proposals to be accepted.

QUESTIONS

1 Find out the meanings of these terms:

  Nationalism
  Home Rule
  Devolution
  Referendum

2 Why do nationalists believe that keeping a linguistic heritage is vital?

3 What have been your own experiences of learning Scottish and Welsh history at secondary school? Is this important?

4 Much more attention is paid today to national feeling in Wales and Scotland. Why do you think this is? Do you think enough is done to respect the distinctiveness of these two nations?

From the Caribbean to Britain

Why did people come to Britain from the Caribbean? What did they find when they arrived here?

Source 25 shows a newspaper advertisement for a ship offering sailings from Jamaica to England. In 1955, 13 ships made 40 sailings on the same run.

There was a combination of reasons why people joined these sailings. Source 26 explains several 'push' factors. The heaviest decade of immigration was between 1950 and 1960. While 15,300 people from the Caribbean arrived in Britain in 1951, that figure had risen to 171,800 by 1961. In 1951, immigrant males outnumbered females by almost two to one, yet by 1961 there was a more even pattern of male–female immigration. What 'pushed' people from the Caribbean to Britain? High unemployment, low wages and rapidly growing populations led some island governments to encourage migration to Britain as a way of reducing their economic problems.

A strong 'pull' factor in many Caribbean people's thinking was the idea that Britain was their 'Mother Country' (see Source 27). Would the Mother Country live up to their expectations? Many looked forward to living in a country where the people would be friendly towards them. There were hints,

SOURCE 26

Housework in Jamaica is really tough. People have to build their own homes from the cheapest material available. There are not many homes with electricity or running water... cooking is done in an outhouse. Water has to be carried and could be some miles away. Firewood has to be gathered. All work has to be done without the aid of machines. Shopping has to be done every day as nothing stays fresh for long.

(A Jamaican woman, Norma Steele, recalls her early life.)

▲ **SOURCE 25**
Newspaper advertisement in the Jamaican *Daily Gleaner*, 8 October 1955.

however, that not all the host population would welcome their arrival.

In the 1950s the Barbados government issued a handbook for emigrants to Britain. It suggested that people in the UK would be less inclined to talk because the British liked to get things done and considered that too much talking was a waste of time. It also suggested that immigrants should learn quickly how British people did things.

Arrival

Source 28 shows a busy scene as newly arrived families gather their belongings to begin new lives in Britain. The men often arrived first and women and children came later, once the man had set up a new home and found a secure job.

Predictably, a big first impression mentioned by many immigrant families was the cold weather. Others recalled the dull light, the size and number of buildings and the vast cities.

SOURCE 27

"There were adverts everywhere: 'Come to the Mother Country! The Mother Country needs you!' I felt strong loyalty to England. There was more emphasis than loyalty to your own island... being away from home wouldn't be that terrible because you would belong.

(A woman, who emigrated to Britain from the Caribbean, recalls her feelings.)"

FOCUS ...*Hyacinth Durrant*

Born in St Vincent in the Caribbean, Hyacinth Durrant was one of the 171,800 West Indians who came to Britain in 1961. She came to join her husband, bringing their young son with her. The journey took 11 days by boat, of which the first three days were spent being sea-sick.
Having left her tropical island 'with sparkling sunshine, mountains, hills and valleys', Hyacinth arrived in London at night. The next day, the reality of the big city dawned:
'... everything looked bleak and depressing ... there were no colours ... just the same bleakish shade'.

A high priority for the Durrant family was finding accommodation, especially after being evicted by their landlord. In their search for accommodation, Hyacinth was faced with direct racial prejudice.
'My three brothers, sister, my husband and myself began a futile search. Almost every room vacant had these words attached to the notices, "No coloureds, no children." I felt rejected by this society.'
Eventually a friend of a friend let the Durrant family rent a single room. In time the council provided them with a larger flat and then a house.

SOURCE 29
Racial prejudice: many immigrants found it difficult to find somewhere to live as landlords discriminated against them.

◄ SOURCE 28
Immigrants arriving at Victoria Station, London, 1956.

The reality of racism

Source 29 is evidence of the racial discrimination that faced many Caribbean immigrants in the 1950s and 1960s. It existed both in jobs and housing. To find themselves, on the one hand, invited by the Mother Country to come to Britain, and then upon arrival to be DISCRIMINATED against by significant numbers of its inhabitants was a shock for which most immigrants had little or no preparation. The British view of Caribbean peoples as a single group failed to understand the complex nature of black people's lives. People with commitments to specific islands settled close to relatives and near local industries, keeping their cultures alive.

The discrimination, together with restrictive legislation on entry and the economic and social difficulties of the 1970s (see page 50), put many black people off. Some returned home. Many who remained brought up children, who as they grew up, resented the inequalities of urban life.

3 **Target Questions**

1 What do Source 26, 28 and the Focus information tell us about the reactions of Caribbean immigrants on first arriving in Britain?

2 Which do you find is the most useful source for answering question 1?

3 These sources only tell us about a few people when, in fact, thousands came. What are the advantages and disadvantages of using sources like these?

4 How would you go about carrying out a more systematic enquiry into these events?

▲ SOURCE 30
The 'Free Nelson Mandela' concert, Wembley Stadium 1988. This was one example of the international pressure put on the South African government to free the black leader Nelson Mandela, who by then had been in prison for 24 years.

SOURCE 31

First, a dominant white group has opposed ... any social or genetic mixing of white with non-white, any sharing of power and any rise of non-whites to positions where they would be superior to whites. In South Africa ... the whites are a dominant minority.

In ... industrially developed countries ... like Britain and the USA, there are minorities distinguished by colour who have migrated to towns seeking work and have found it hard to get except the lowest paid and most unpleasant. They ... get caught in a vicious circle of bad housing, bad schools and poor jobs from which it is difficult to escape.

(Philip Mason)

A world perspective on civil rights

How has the struggle for civil rights for black people been carried on in other countries?

The unexpected hostility which faced many black immigrants to Britain were examples of racial prejudice and discrimination. Such attitudes were certainly not new, nor were they confined to Britain. Racial discrimination and the quest for civil rights by minority groups comes in many different forms around the world. Source 30 is just one particular case. Source 31 provides the context for the two area studies on these pages.

SOURCE 32

We, the people of South Africa, declare, for all our country and the world to know that South Africa belongs to all who live in it, black and white, and that no government can justly claim authority unless it is based on the will of the people.

(From the Freedom Charter 1955, drawn up to proclaim the basis of a democratic, multi-racial South Africa. This idea was crushed for 35 years, but is getting closer now.)

Apartheid in South Africa
Racial inequality has been practised in South Africa for centuries. The Dutch farmers (or 'Boers') seized land from black Africans in the 17th century. White domination meant white prosperity at the expense of black Africans. The 1913 Land Act said it was illegal for blacks to own land outside their own areas, and kept most of the land for whites. Black workers would be regarded as 'migrant' labour, paid low wages and given no political or civil rights.

When the Nationalist government began APARTHEID in 1945, white domination was well-established. Apartheid simply made it more systematic. Black South Africans were deprived of all their civil rights. There were harsh laws: the main opposition party, the African National Congress (ANC) was banned, leaders could be arrested without trial and violent police action was used. Black leaders like Nelson Mandela (Source 30) were imprisoned. Mandela had helped draw up the 1955 Freedom Charter (see Source 32).

South Africa found itself increasingly isolated by the world community. Economic trade sanctions imposed by many Western nations eventually began to take effect. Since 1990 things have begun to change. Nelson Mandela was released and some of the apartheid laws abolished. The white government started power-sharing talks with the ANC. Elections in which all can vote are to be held in April 1994.

Civil rights in the USA
Since 1870, the USA has, in theory, been a society of equality between the races. In fact, however, especially in the South where most black Americans lived, there was extreme prejudice and discrimination. The Ku Klux Klan (see Source 33) practised racial hatred. Even the army, navy and air force were segregated.

Unlike South Africa, however, the post-war US government did begin to tackle the problem. In 1948, the armed forces were integrated. Racially segregated schools were declared illegal in 1954. In 1957 President Eisenhower called in troops to protect black pupils entering previously all-white schools.

Protests at white resistance to equality increased during the 1960s. Martin Luther King, an inspirational leader, raised the profile of the peaceful civil rights campaign. King's message (see Source 34) was for equality through non-violent protest. After his assassination in 1968, other 'black power' civil rights leaders like Stokeley Carmichael and Malcolm X took a stronger stance against the authorities in pursuit of equal rights for black citizens. Some progress was made in the 1970s and 1980s, with the arrival of a large, successful black middle class. But for many US citizens, to be black is to be poor and to be poor is to suffer from a greater loss of civil rights.

The struggle goes on

The issue of civil rights, based on equality of opportunity, is a continuing struggle. As the Cold War ended there was optimistic talk of a 'new world order'. But events in the world's trouble spots seem increasingly to be based upon issues of racial and religious hatred. Today, even after the HOLOCAUST, the spectre of 'ethnic cleansing' hangs over many parts of Europe, Asia and Africa.

◄ **SOURCE 33**
The Ku Klux Klan (KKK) was a secret society of Americans dedicated to maintaining white supremacy. Its tactics of terror against black Americans included beatings, burnings and lynchings. By the 1920s the KKK boasted 4 million members. Although illegal, the Klan still survives at local level in some parts of the southern states.

SOURCE 34

On 20 August 1963, nearly 500,000 people marched into Washington to hear Martin Luther King. This is an extract from his speech:

I have a dream that my four little children one day will live in a nation where they will not be judged by the colour of their skin. So let freedom ring from ... every state and every city ... to speed up that day when all of God's children, black and white, ... will be able to join hands and sing, ... 'Free at last! ... Great God Almighty, we are free at last!.'

QUESTIONS

1   **The struggle for civil rights in South Africa and the USA has taken a long time to achieve anything. Why has it taken so long?**

2   **What part do each of the following play in a civil rights movement: inspirational leaders; mass support; international support; the mass media?**

3   **What are the arguments for and against non-violent protest, as opposed to the use of violence?**

Multi-cultural Britain

What are some of your favourite meals? Do you associate any of them with particular countries? The popularity of many of the dishes shown in Source 35 is, to a large degree, a consequence of the migration to Britain by significant numbers of people from other parts of the world.

Migration to Britain is nothing new. As the time chart on page 80 shows, Britain's population has long been made up of a multi-cultural blend of peoples. The actual numbers of people from ethnic minorities within modern Britain is not that great: 2,580,000 people in 1991, or 4.7 per cent of the total population. Nevertheless, the range of cultures is very wide. Over 130 languages were spoken by different pupils

▲ SOURCE 36
Enoch Powell.

in London schools in 1978.

During the 1960s and 1970s both of the main political parties had the same approach to race relations and the law: immigration should be controlled and racial discrimination should be attacked (see information box). Unfortunately, the aims of the second were made harder by the first. Immigration control was clearly carried out on the basis of colour and race. White South Africans, for instance, could enter Britain even though South Africa left the Commonwealth in 1961. British passport holders from black Commonwealth countries, by contrast, could not. Such racially based policies made it harder to break down prejudice against black Britons through laws such as the Race Relations Acts.

There was also the implication that immigration was a 'problem' which had to be reduced. The problems faced by migrants to Britain were those of discrimination in employment and housing based on racial prejudice. It was usual for first generation immigrants to face difficulties of acceptance among the host population.

Enoch Powell (Source 36) inflamed some of these prejudices by warning that because of immigration British cities might be faced with 'rivers of blood': in other words race riots similar to those in the USA. He suggested that immigrants should be REPATRIATED to their home countries. Since the 1970s there has been a varied picture in race relations in Britain. On the one hand, black people have made an increasing contribution to British life, through the arts (see Source 37), sport, important fields of employment such as the NHS, and many other areas.

SOURCE 35 ►
A sample of different meals introduced by immigrants to Britain.

LEGISLATION	
IMMIGRATION CONTROL	**RACE RELATIONS**
Commonwealth Immigration Act 1962 People, even with British passports, could only enter Britain if they had a work permit. Those who had British parents or grandparents could enter freely (i.e. mostly whites).	**Race Relations Act 1965** Made it illegal to practise discrimination in pubs, restaurants and hotels. Also illegal to stir up racial hatred. Set up the Race Relations Board.
Commonwealth Immigration Act 1968 Put restrictions on British passport holders of Asian origin who were living in Africa where they were often persecuted.	**Race Relations Act 1968** Gave more powers to the Race Relations Board.
Immigration Act 1971 Defined 'patrial' as those born in Britain, or who had a parent or grandparent born in Britain. Only patrials could come and go freely.	**Race Relations Act 1976** Set up the Commission for Racial Equality.

On the other hand, Britain experienced serious economic difficulties in the 1970s. There were strikes, unemployment and a widening of the gap between 'haves' and 'have-nots' (see page 62). In these situations ethnic groups are often unfairly blamed and become visible targets for race hatred. Source 39 shows white youths, often under the dubious patronage of ultra-right wing political organisations like the British National Party and National Front. Young black youths reacted to the slow progress towards equality of opportunity and outright hostility from some sections of white society. The 1970s ended with riots in parts of some inner-city areas, including Bristol, London and Liverpool.

Nevertheless, as Source 38 suggests, as Britain moves towards the 21st century, its multi-racial nature is a fact of life, and the British people cannot be thought of in terms of a single racial group.

SOURCE 37 ➤
The 1975 production of *The Black Mikado* was a hit with London audiences. Black performers were making a growing impact in all branches of show business during the 1970s. Television in particular was doing more to reflect the views, tastes and talents of the black community.

▲ SOURCE 39
In Lewisham, south London, a National Front demonstration on 13 August 1977 presented the police with the difficult task of keeping the peace.

SOURCE 38

The problems facing blacks in Britain are varied and became clearer to the wider population in the aftermath of the 1981 riots. But many are problems not of their making; they are in fact difficulties of adjustment and policy among the white host society.

The future population trends are clear. Whatever the points of conflict, black Britons are entitled to the full range of rights enjoyed by whites. The future harmony of British life depends in large measure in securing that basic objective.

(Extract from *A Passage to Britain*, December 1986.)

1 *Target Questions*

Consider these scenarios. What might the reaction be of each person to the situation? Explain your answer.

1 *A senior police officer faced with deciding if a proposed National Front march, through an area with a largely black population, should go ahead.*

2 *A white policeman faced with keeping order at a National Front demonstration.*

3 *A black doctor faced with a white casualty arising out of violence at a National Front demonstration.*

4 *A black policeman faced with duty near the route of a National Front demonstration.*

5 *A black community leader faced with issuing advice on a forthcoming National Front demonstration.*

From empire

In the introduction to this book, you saw that European countries and their empires dominated the world. In this unit you will find out how European countries felt about their empires and why they eventually granted, or were forced to grant, independence to them.

The destruction caused by war and the loss of their empires persuaded several Western European countries that they should join together, perhaps even becoming one state. You will find out how they did this and how Britain relates to this movement.

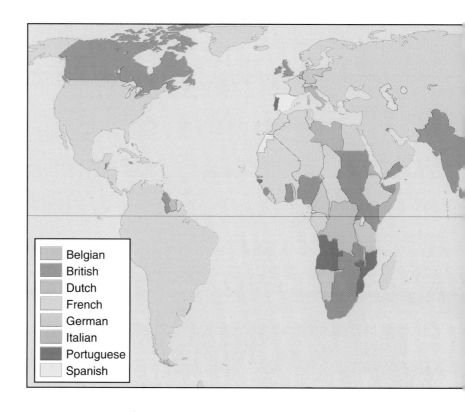

Belgian
British
Dutch
French
German
Italian
Portuguese
Spanish

Key Questions

What were the causes of the end of the British, French and other empires?

Why and how has Europe become united?

Why did it take so long for Britain to become a member of the EEC?

Source 1 shows the way European empires covered most of the globe in 1914. Even in Latin America and China, European countries such as Britain, Spain, Portugal and Germany had big investments and so wielded a lot of influence. The prosperity, power and status of several European countries depended on ruling these empires.

For reasons you can read about in this unit, these empires came to an end after 1945. The two world wars left Europe exhausted and divided. By 1945, as you will see in unit 7, the world was dominated by the new superpowers, the USA and USSR. Where did that leave the nations of Europe?

For a number of important people in France, Italy, Germany and the Benelux countries, the answer was European unity. Very soon after the end of the war they started to plan, first in key areas of heavy industry, then in other areas where co-operation was worthwhile, then in all aspects of trade. These movements are explained in detail in this unit.

This movement for unity in Europe has been spectacularly successful. The economies of the European Community states have grown and the vision of a united Europe is widely supported in mainland Europe. To most politicians and most people the proposed next move, the creation of one state and

◀ **SOURCE 1**
The world in 1914.

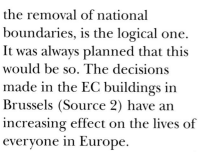

SOURCE 2 ▶
The headquarters building of the European Community Secretariat, Brussels.

> Time was slipping by, and my attempt to create a nucleus around which a European Community might be formed met with no response from the one great power in Europe which was then in a position to take such a responsibility (Britain).
>
> (From Jean Monnet's *Memoirs*.)
>
> When, on our return we put these proposals to Bevin [Foreign Secretary in the Labour government], they were immediately rejected, as Bevin felt that they went too far in the direction of a surrender of British sovereignty.
>
> (From Edwin Plowden's *Memoirs*.)

▲ **SOURCE 3**
Reports of a high-level meeting held in April 1949 between Jean Monnet, French foreign minister, and Edwin Plowden of the British delegation.

the removal of national boundaries, is the logical one. It was always planned that this would be so. The decisions made in the EC buildings in Brussels (Source 2) have an increasing effect on the lives of everyone in Europe.

Britain has never been sure about this. Source 1 shows that the British Empire was by far the largest of the European empires. When key meetings like the one referred to in Source 3 were being held in 1949, Britain still had an empire. Britain had not been invaded during the Second World War, either. As Source 3 shows, Edwin Plowden and Ernest Bevin clearly did not share the vision of the future

put forward by Jean Monnet. To be fair, sinking Britain's lot with the shattered countries of Europe must have seemed a slightly crazy idea in 1949.

The British Commonwealth was an idea put forward after the First World War. It formally came into existence in 1931, by the Statute of Westminster. It was meant to be an organisation of equals. At first, its members were Britain, Canada, Australia, New Zealand and South Africa – a 'white man's club'. As former colonies have gained independence, most have joined the Commonwealth. It is still an organisation of equals, with the Queen at its head, but now the membership is multi-racial. Members find it useful to meet and talk; it encourages

trading, cultural and educational links.

In no sense has the Commonwealth replaced the Empire. Even by the 1960s it was clear that Britain's future lay with Europe. Since 1973 Britain has been a member of the EC, but has never really shared in Monnet's vision. The loss of sovereignty (that is the right to have the final say in matters affecting your own country) worried Bevin in 1949 and worried Margaret Thatcher in the 1980s. The British seem reluctant Europeans. They seem slower than most to switch from being a great imperial power to accepting present realities. Is this the fault of history? Or of how people think about their history?

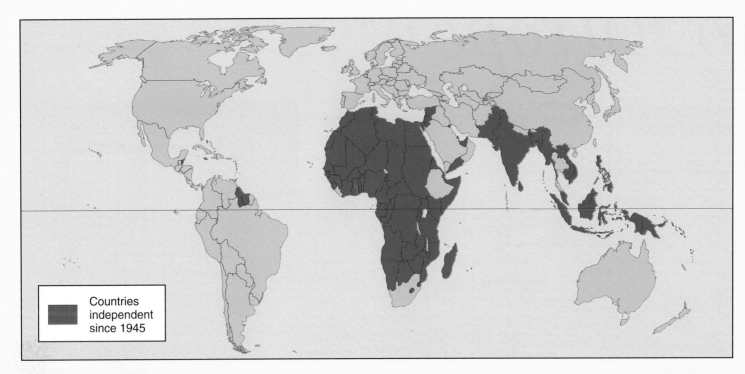

The world transformed

Look at Source 4, and contrast it with Source 1 on page 96. The difference between them is dramatic. In 1945, the world was divided into just 70 states. By 1985, there were over 170 independent self-governing nations, each ruling its own people in its own way. Why, and how, has this world-wide transformation taken place? What have been its results?

Retreat from empire

The major cause of this dramatic change has been the collapse, since 1945, of the European COLONIAL empires that formerly controlled a large part of the world. Why did these countries give up their empires?

Put simply, there were four main reasons: problems and pressures at home; changing attitudes among the rulers and the ruled; the rise of an educated ÉLITE among colonised peoples; and demands for independence by the colonies themselves (see pages 100 to 107).

Independence was not always willingly granted. There have been many wars between European governments and their colonies since 1945. Two struggles for freedom, in India and Algeria, are looked at in more detail on pages 104, 105 and 107.

A legacy of unrest?

You can see the moment one colony gained independence recorded in Source 5. Yet the proud hopes suggested by that photograph have not always been fufilled. Tragically, many new nations soon became engulfed in bitter fighting, either with their neighbours, or in bloody CIVIL WARS. Source 6 shows what happened in the vast, powerful African state of Nigeria, between 1967 and 1970. Some historians have suggested that wars were almost bound to happen in colonial nations after independence. Look at the data in the information box for reasons why.

A legacy of poverty?

European colonial empires were run for the economic benefit of the ruling country. Sometimes, this brought prosperity to certain groups of local people (merchants in India for example) but usually it had a bad effect on the economy of the colony itself. Colonies were used to provide cheap, unskilled labour and raw materials. Ways of ending poverty and creating wealth, such as

▲ **SOURCE 4**
Colonies and former colonies in 1990.

▲ **SOURCE 5**
The independence ceremony for another British colony: Northern Rhodesia becomes Zambia, 1964.

PROBLEMS FACING FORMER COLONIES

Europeans' colonial boundaries ignored traditional ethnic, religious and language groupings. This led to civil wars. Examples: Nigeria, Rwanda.

Traditional lifestyles had been replaced by Western-style institutions. Some local people felt these were not right for their country. Examples: Tanzania, Libya.

Many ex-colonies were very poor, and had little chance of getting richer. Examples: Chad, Sudan.

Rich colonies had the potential to become powerful, but rival groups (or outsiders) tried to seize their assets. Examples: Zaire, Kuwait.

Ex-colonies were vulnerable to takeover by extremist political groups (left or right wing). Examples: Angola, Vietnam.

1 *In Source 7, Gandhi suggested that colonial government might sometimes be good for a country. What evidence is there in the sources and text on these pages of benefits brought by colonisation?*

2 *Can you find examples of harm done by colonial rule?*

3 *Gandhi also suggested that independent governments might be bad. What do you think he meant by this?*

4 *What evidence is there to suggest that some of the problems facing former colonies today might not be their present governments' fault?*

SOURCE 7

No people exists that would rather not think itself happier under its own bad government than it might be under the good government of an alien power.

(Mohandas Gandhi, Indian campaigner for freedom and justice, said this in 1905.)

◣ SOURCE 6
In 1967 the Ibo people in south-east Nigeria declared themselves independent of the rest of the country and set up a republic called Biafra. Troops from the rest of Nigeria fought the Biafrans, and cut off food supplies, causing famine and starvation for many ordinary people. This photograph shows the aftermath of an air attack by Nigerian jets on the Biafran town of Umuahia, 1968.

education and training, improved farming methods, or industrial and commercial development, were often ignored.

As a result, most new, post-colonial nations have found it difficult to compete in the world market-place with the older, industrialised nations of Europe and America, or the new Far Eastern economic powers (Japan, Hong Kong, South Korea and Taiwan). The prices of the raw materials they produce often vary widely. Many former colonies are also situated in lands where the climate is harsh and unhealthy. As a result they have often found themselves unable to manage their economies and feed their peoples without borrowing money from their former colonial rulers. This has led to worrying burdens of debt: in some countries, overseas debt repayments make up the largest item in the national budget, leaving little to spend on development at home. In

1965, Kwame Nkrumah, leader of newly independent Ghana, called this burden of debt 'neo-colonialism' (new colonialism).

Freedom and dignity
In spite of these problems, the end of empire did bring some benefits. Wealthy, white nations no longer assume they have a God-given right to rule over people of other colours, or that they 'know best' how to run the world. Statesmen who campaigned for colonial freedom, such as Julius Nyerere (born 1921) of Tanzania, Jomo Kenyatta (1893–1978) of Kenya, Mohandas Gandhi (1869–1948) and Jawarharlal Nehru (1889–1964), both of India, have won widespread respect. And, after almost a century of struggle, the world has come to accept the principle of self-government put forward by Gandhi in 1905 (see Source 7) that people have the right to run their own countries and their own lives.

Power and glory?

In 1902, a British journalist, A.C. Benson, wrote a patriotic song. It was set to music by Sir Edward Elgar (1857–1934), a leading British composer, and became immensely popular. This is how it began:

> Land of Hope and Glory, Mother of the Free,
> How shall we extol thee, who are born of thee?
> Wider still and wider, shall thy bounds be set;
> God who made the mighty, make thee mightier yet.

Today, many British people enjoy Elgar's rousing tune, and do not worry about what the words mean. But, at the time Benson wrote this song, his words were treated seriously, and with approval. The British empire was at the height of its power, and people wanted to celebrate that fact.

SOURCE 8

The views of some British men about the empire.

'It may be that some of these peoples [Malays, Dyaks, Chinese] were restive under British rule, but there was no outward sign of it. The British gave them justice, provided them with hospitals and schools, and encouraged their industries. There was no more crime than anywhere else.'

(Somerset Maugham, writer and traveller, describing the 1920s and 1930s.)

'I don't believe any of us believed that British rule would come to an end...'

(Eugene Pierce, son of a British railway manager in India.)

'I'm quite certain that colonialism was a good thing from the point of view of the African native himself. It taught him respect of the law, it removed him from the constant fear of witchcraft and it taught him also that you could have a democratic government instead of the absolute rule of the chiefs.'

(Sir Alan Burns, British administrator in Nigeria 1912 to 1942.)

'Undoubtedly we interfered with the Africans, sometimes by trying to introduce our own way of life which didn't suit them...'

(Sir Gerald Reece, British administrator in East Africa 1925 to 1953.)

◄ **SOURCE 9**
British District Officer in the Sudan, 1950s.

SOURCE 10

There were petty court cases, there were matters connected with the African courts, there were things connected with the prison. But there was also road-building, tree planting, the collection of tax, the exemption of tax from some of the older people or the sick; there were things like trading licences, matters connected with hygiene and extension of the health service which the medical officer couldn't possibly cope with himself. All this together with endless miscellaneous things connected with schools, churches, and various individual things that people would bring forward because they rightly regarded the DO as the person to whom to bring their complaints and their problems.

(Sir Frank Loyd was a District Officer (DO) in Tangyanika (now Tanzania) in the 1940s.)

Why was there an empire?

There are several possible answers to this question. First and foremost, because British people believed that it was good. Source 8 should help you understand this point of view. It contains opinions expressed by British people who ran the empire during the early years of this century. What did they believe the empire was trying to achieve? Source 9 shows British administration in action and Source 10 tells us how one typical official managed 'his' part of the empire.

The second reason why British people supported the empire was also a matter of belief. As Benson's song shows, many people believed that the British empire was somehow 'approved' by God. If it wasn't, they argued, He would never have let it develop. This way of thinking is not very common today, but it was powerful in the past. Christian MISSIONARIES felt it was their duty to carry this 'superior' faith to the rest of the empire. However, many missionaries also helped local peoples by providing medical care and education.

What did the British feel about their empire? Who gained from the empire?

"Imperialism probably remained a core ideology in British society well into the 1950s, when a last generation of schoolchildren were raised on the moral certainties of imperial rule through history textbooks, geography lessons, Empire Day (a public holiday), children's literature and popular cinema."

(Historian John Schofield, 1992.)

Imperial self-image

Source 11 reveals that the mixture of British self-confidence and religion was a powerful and long-lasting one. It may even have had a stronger effect on British culture at home than it did abroad.

Who gained from the empire?

The empire was not all about bringing 'civilisation' or Christianity. It was also about power. Owning an empire gave Britain status and influence among other countries.

There was rivalry between European nations to see whose empire was biggest and best. Many British colonies, especially in Africa and Asia, were strategically important. Britain needed to hold on to them to stop new conquests by rivals, and to maintain communications links between home and overseas.

'Trade follows the flag'

Around 1900, people believed that business and commerce followed political control of the empire. For a few colonies, it might have been true. But in many cases, trade came before 'the flag', or they went hand in hand. With hindsight, we might almost say that the empire had been set up simply to benefit Britain economically. Like other European nations, Britain looked at its colonies as assets, to be exploited. They provided valuable raw materials (tin, gold, diamonds, copper, rubber, wool, cotton) for British industry, and vital foodstuffs (sugar, tea, wheat, lamb, beef and butter) to feed the British people.

The vast colonial populations held out the promise of profitable new markets for British manufactured goods, and there were rich opportunities for British businessmen to invest in colonial mines, ranches and farms. Source 12 shows British managers supervising workers on a rubber plantation in Malaya. What similarities are there between it and Source 2?

▲ **SOURCE 12**
British managers and workers on a rubber plantation in Malaya in the 1940s.

(2) Target Questions

1 Look at the evidence of the impact of colonial rule on colonised countries in Sources 9, 10 and 12. Which gives the most factual information? Which gives the most information about ideas and opinions?

2 Which of the views in Source 8 do you think best describes the attitudes of the British to colonialism?

3 Source 11 was written by a modern historian. How far do the sources and text on these pages support his view of British imperialism?

4 Look at the names and jobs held by the authors of the comments in Source 8. How far does this information help to explain what they are saying?

5 Why is it difficult to find out exactly what the reasons for British imperialism were?

The end of empire

Why did the European empires come to an end?

In 1920, the government of the British empire controlled the lives of more than 600 million people, in lands covering one quarter of the earth's surface. Stretching round the world from North Africa to New Zealand to Newfoundland, it was truly an empire 'on which the sun never set'.

Yet, by 1970, Britain had almost no colonies. The same was true of other European empires. France, Belgium, the Netherlands, Italy and Spain had all handed over most of their colonial lands to independent national rule.

Why had this happened? There is no simple reason; instead, a number of events and trends worked together to put pressure on the old imperial powers. The sources on these pages will help you to find out what they were.

▲ **SOURCE 13**
Japanese guarding British troops taken prisoner after the fall of Singapore, 1942.

The world at war

Source 13 shows British soldiers surrendering to Japanese troops after the capture of Singapore by the Japanese army in 1942. Look back to Source 9 on page 100. Contrast the brash confidence expressed by British imperial rulers with their situation in this picture. Britain and the other colonial powers, with American help, eventually defeated the Japanese and regained their colonial lands. However, the fact that empire troops could be captured in battle, and their lands conquered, caused an immense loss of prestige. What price 'hope and glory' now?

The Japanese conquerors were harsh, but, from colonial peoples' point of view, was this really that much different from European rule? There was still no independence for colonised lands. Japanese officials who replaced the defeated British and French in Malaya, Burma and Indo-China shrewdly invented the slogan 'Asia for the Asians', to win support among conquered peoples.

The Indian nationalist leader, Subhas Chandra Bose (1897–1945) even formed an army to fight with the Japanese against Britain. He thought India stood a better chance of winning independence that way.

Superpowers

Britain and Europe were exhausted by the war. They had used all their money for troops and weapons. Commerce and industry had been disrupted. Homes, railways, shops and factories had been flattened by bombs. International trade was in a mess. Did they still need their empires? Could they still afford to keep them? Two new superpowers, the USA and the USSR, were emerging from the post-war chaos. Both were critical of imperialism. In the future they, and not Britain, would rule the world.

A new ruling class

Source 14 illustrates another key factor in the collapse of empire: the growth of an educated élite, drawn from colonial countries themselves.

People are a country's most important resource, but practical facilities such as roads, railways, schools and hospitals (often called the 'infrastructure') are important, too. Under imperial rule, these had been built in colonial lands, sometimes for the first time. They were of tremendous value. As early as 1927, British engineers had constructed over 92,000 km of road in India and thousands of kilometres of railway track.

F⊙CUS ...*Léopold Senghor*

The career of Léopold Sédar Senghor is typical of those educated people who led their countries to independence from imperial rule.

Senghor was born in 1906 to a peasant family in Senegal, a French colony in West Africa. After an education at the local mission school, he attended university in Paris and worked as a schoolteacher. He became famous as a writer and as a campaigner for black peoples' rights.

He played an active part in French and Senegalese politics, and, after Senegal became independent in 1960, ruled as its first president until he retired in 1980.

▲ SOURCE 14
Educated colonial élite: lawyers in the Gold Coast (now Ghana), 1930s.

▼ SOURCE 16
Anti-British agitation: protests for the independence of Southern Rhodesia (now Zimbabwe) in 1963.

New attitudes

Source 15 reveals some of the changes in social attitudes that were taking place in Europe. In the 1940s, Hitler's treatment of the Jews as a 'subject race' shocked many people. They became aware of racism and its dangers, perhaps for the first time. Britain's stand against Hitler won great respect. But how could the country which championed freedom and tolerance justify ruling an empire of its own?

Above all, European empires came to an end because local peoples wanted them to. Sometimes independence was arranged peacefully by negotiation; at other times, it was only achieved after bloodshed. In the long run, however, it was impossible for an imperial administration to keep control of a country against its will. Nationalist feeling helped unite the different peoples within a colony against their colonial ruler.

In the same way, colonial governments could not hope to succeed against freedom fighters who had the support of the local population. Source 16 shows the aftermath of an attack by members of the Mau Mau secret society in Kenya. The Mau Mau were condemned for their terrorist tactics. They killed at least 95 white settlers and over 1,920 Africans. British attempts to control them failed, and Kenya eventually gained its independence.

By the 1960s, at least some European governments realised that the time had come to give up their empires. The world had changed.

SOURCE 15

"The whole structure seemed to be very different after World War II...we decided that we would spend much of our time getting to know the new élite. We were convinced that this was where the future lay.... I'm not blaming people for not doing this before the war. I think in that kind of society – both European society and the Colonial service hierarchical society – this would have been impossible."

(Anthony Kirk-Greene, British administrator in Nigeria, 1950–1961.)

1 *Target Questions*

1 *Make two lists of the results of the Second World War in Britain under these headings: 'practical results' and 'psychological results'.*

2 *Make two more lists, of the results of these events in the colonies, under the headings: 'short-term results' and 'long-term results'.*

3 *Give each of the changes on the lists a score (rated 1 to 5) depending how important you think each one was as a cause of Britain deciding to give up its empire. Which are the most important?*

How did India achieve independence?

For many years, Britons liked to think of India as 'the jewel in the crown' of their empire. Images like Source 17, showing a serenely powerful VICEROY, were stirring and reassuring. Yet this highly prized 'jewel' was the first British colony to be granted independence, in 1947. Why?

'Swaraj'

Even before Queen Victoria was declared Empress of India in 1876, Indian people had begun to demand the right to take part in government. The time chart on the page opposite shows the main stages in the Indian independence campaign. From it, you can see that the first demands for Indian *swaraj* (home rule) were made in 1916, and regularly thereafter. But the British government did not want to listen.

Source 18 reveals some typical British attitudes in the years before 1947. Eventually, many Britons came to change their minds. This was mainly the result of an UNORTHODOX campaign waged by an extraordinary man, Mohandas Gandhi (1869–1948).

FOCUS *...Mohandas Gandhi*

Gandhi leads protesters on the 'Salt March', 1931.

1869 Born Porbandar, India, father: government official; mother: deeply religious.

1889 To Britain to train as a lawyer.

1891 Qualifies and returns to India.

1893–1915 Works as lawyer in South Africa. Develops philosophy of non-violent protest, called *satyagraha*; wins campaigns for civil rights. Given the title 'Mahatma' (Great Soul) by his followers.

1915 Returns to India; calls for independence and for reform of Hindu faith. Demands equality for the 'untouchables' – the lowest rank in Hindu society.

1917–1947 Campaigns tirelessly; his 'weapons' include protest marches, strikes, fasting and silence. Put in prison many times. Patiently negotiates with British government.

1947 Welcomes Independence, but is saddened by the division of India and by the violent riots.

1948 Killed by Hindu assassin.

▲ **SOURCE 17**
Lord Louis Mountbatten, the last Viceroy of India, with his wife Edwina, 1946.

> **SOURCE 18**
>
> Some British opinions about India:
>
> 'The English never cared, the politicians especially. I don't think they ever took any interest in India at all.'
> (Field-Marshal Sir Claude Auchinleck, Supreme Commander, British Army in India 1947.)
>
> 'As long as we rule India, we are the greatest power in the world. If we lose it, we shall drop straight away to a third-rate power.'
> (Viceroy of India 1900.)
>
> 'They were there for a very good reason; earning a living and making money – nothing ignoble about that – but I don't feel that most people had a sense of vocation, that they were serving India.'
> (John Morris, British army officer in India 1916 to 1930.)
>
> 'I thought nothing about the Raj...I had a job... and that was all there was to it.'
> (Norman Watney, British railway manager in India, 1925 to 1946.)

A sense of destiny

You can read about Gandhi's campaign in the Focus box. Gandhi did not act alone. He worked closely with the Indian National Congress Party (founded 1885) to try and negotiate independence by peaceful agreement. But the British moved slowly in these talks, and, it seemed, reluctantly. Look again at Source 18: do the opinions there help to explain why? The Indian leaders were determined; they shared a strong sense of the rightness of their cause, together with a sense of destiny.

Gandhi's life and work, dedicated to non-violence, showed that what he called *satyagraha* (the power of truth) could be a strong weapon. His hunger strikes and protest marches gained widespread publicity. But, in the end, violence played a crucial role in fixing the date for India's independence. In 1942, when Japanese troops were poised to invade, Congress announced an anti-British 'Quit India' campaign, and there were widespread riots, in which thousands of people were killed. The army stayed loyal to Britain, and fought bravely against the Japanese, but it was a terrible warning of what might happen if Indian demands were not met.

Time chart

INDIA 1857–1948

1857 Mutiny by soldiers of British East India Company, which controlled much of India.
1858 British government takes over.
1876 Queen Victoria declared Empress of India.
1885 Indian National Congress Party formed.
1906 Muslim League (political party) formed.
1914–1918 Indians fight bravely for Britain in the First World War. Some hope for independence as a reward.
1916 Campaign for *swaraj* (home rule) begins.
1917 Britain promises 'responsible government for India as part of Empire'.
1919 Amritsar Massacre – British troops kill 379 unarmed protesters.
1920 Gandhi starts peaceful protest campaigns.
1930 Start of Round Table Conference (London) on home rule; talks later break down.
1935 Britain passes Government of India Act; more Indians than before can now vote.

1939 Second World War; Britain involves India in fighting without asking permission. Gandhi is outraged.
1940 Muslim League demands separate Muslim states.
1941 12,000 Congress leaders imprisoned.
1942 Japan conquers Burma (neighbouring British colony).
1942 Britain promises India independence after the war, in exchange for Indian support in the war. Congress replies with 'Quit India' campaign. Riots.
1945 War ends; Britain agrees independence, but violent Hindu/Muslim clashes over Partition.
1947 India and Pakistan independent. Many deaths as 14 million refugees seek new homes in Hindu or Muslim territories.

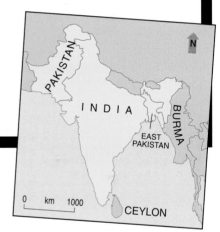

SOURCE 19

You British people, you're good administrators, but you are very bad psychologists. You talk about Indian nationality but there is no such thing. I don't regard the Hindus as my fellow nationals at all, and they don't regard me as their fellow national. You talk about democracy, but you know that there was never any such thing as democracy in India before you came. ... It will pass with you.

(Reported to have been said by Muhammad Ali Jinnah in 1946.)

QUESTIONS

1 Why do you think Indian people accepted British independence for so long?

2 Why do you think fighting finally broke out in 1942?

3 When you look at the opinions in Source 18, why is it difficult to reach a conclusion about the British people who ruled India?

Partition

In 1945, Britain finally agreed to Indian independence. But the violence was not over; in fact, it got worse. Out of an Indian population of 600 million, 90 million were Muslim. Led by Muhammad Ali Jinnah (1876–1948), this Muslim minority refused to join a united, independent India. Instead, they wanted a separate Muslim state of their own. You can read Jinnah's reasons in Source 19. While this was being discussed, tension mounted, and there were violent clashes between the Hindu and Muslim communities. Almost half a million people were killed.

Britain agreed to divide colonial India into two new nations, India and Pakistan, as quickly as possible in order to prevent further fighting. They both became independent in 1947.

Letting go

Why did many colonies have to fight for independence?

In 1960, the British Prime Minister, Harold Macmillan, spoke about a 'wind of change' sweeping through Africa, which the British empire could not resist (Source 20). This was his way of saying, tactfully, that Britain realised it could no longer control developments in many of its colonies. Britain had therefore decided to 'give in gracefully', and grant independence to most of those colonies that remained. But did Macmillan's words tell the whole story? Compare them with the more outspoken comments in Source 21.

Not everyone shared Macmillan's views. Many European governments were reluctant to give up their colonies. Some wanted to hold on to overseas possessions for economic gain. For example, Belgium did not want to lose the mineral-rich territory of the Congo (now Zaire) (see page 135). Others wanted to stop the spread of political views which they opposed. France fought fiercely against communist rebels in Vietnam (see page 130) and Britain defeated communists in Malaya.

A few colonial rulers, like the Portuguese president, Antonio de Salazar (1889–1970), opposed nationalism of any kind. These political differences between colonial governments and the peoples they governed often led to war, as you can see from the time chart.

Fighting for freedom

The richest and most important French colony was Algeria, and the Algerian War (1954–1962) was the most bitter and savage of all the conflicts that accompanied the end of imperial rule. It led to the deaths of over 20,000 French soldiers and settlers, plus 1 million Algerian civilians, and almost

SOURCE 20

"We have seen the awakening of national consciousness in peoples who have for centuries lived in dependence on some foreign power. ... A wind of change is blowing through this continent, whether we like it or not.

(Harold Macmillan, speech to the South African Parliament, 3 February 1960.)"

caused a revolution in France. Even today, a legacy of sadness and suspicion remains. Why did this terrible conflict take place?

'Pieds noirs'

Algeria was different. Since 1860, many thousands of French settlers, sometimes called *pieds noirs* (black feet), had gone to live and work there. This large settler community was unknown in most other colonies, where the European residents were outnumbered by a much larger local population. In India, for example, the 1901 census recorded 300 million Indians but only 900 British civil servants and about 70,000 British troops. As one British administrator commented: 'If the Indians all spit at once, we shall be drowned.'

COLONIAL WARS 1945–1990		
Date	Location	Colonial power
1945–1947	India	Britain
1945–1949	Indonesia	Netherlands
1946–1947	Palestine	Britain*
1946–1954	Vietnam	France
1947	Madagascar	France
1948–1960	Malaya	Britain
1952–1956	Tunisia	France
1952–1960	Kenya	Britain
1953–1956	Morocco	France
1956	Cameroon	France
1954–1962	Algeria	France
1958–1967	Aden/Yemen	Britain
1961–1975	Angola	Portugal
1963–1974	Guinea-Bissau	Portugal
1964–1974	Mozambique	Portugal
1965–1979	Rhodesia/Zimbabwe	Britain†
1975	Western Sahara	Spain

* Britain ruled Palestine under a Mandate (authority) from the Paris Peace Conference, held at the end of the First World War. Legally, it was not a colony, but was governed rather like one.

† In 1965 the Rhodesian government declared itself independent from Britain. Black groups seeking majority rule then fought a war with the Rhodesian authorities.

SOURCE 21

Independence... was suddenly rushing upon us at breakneck speed – but at a speed which could not be slowed down at all without the risk of the most violent bloodshed and disruption.

(Charles Meek, British administrator in Tanganyika (Tanzania) in 1958.)

◀ **SOURCE 22**
Rich and poor in
Algeria: French
Algerians in an Algiers
street café give money
to an ethnic Algerian
beggar, 1940s.

Colonial citizens

By 1954, the descendants of the original
settlers in Algeria numbered over a million.
Algeria was their home; they had been born
there. Many thought of themselves as the
'real' Algerians, and treated local people as
second-class citizens. *Pieds noirs* occupied
the top jobs, and received the best
education. And, although all French
colonial subjects, whatever their race, were
equal in the eyes of the law, in practice only
the *pieds noirs* had full civil rights. In 1919
the French government gave ethnic Algerian
people the right to vote and take part in
politics, but only if they abandoned their
traditional faith, Islam. Understandably,
most did not.

There was another source of tension.
The *pieds noirs* were richer than the local
people (Source 22); many hoped to become
even more prosperous after vast oil deposits
were discovered in 1952. This gap between
rich and poor caused resentment, and there
were demonstrations by Algerian protesters
throughout the 1930s and 1940s.

A 'French Algeria'?

War broke out in 1954, when the Algerian
Liberation Front (FLN – *Front de Libération
Nationale*) organised bombings and terrorist
attacks throughout the country. *Pieds noirs*
and French soldiers alike were brutally
killed (Source 23). Faced with horrified
public opinion at home, the French
government decided to fight to preserve 'a
French Algeria'. But when news leaked out
that French armed forces had been
torturing suspected FLN members, and
destroying their homes, there was an outcry.
Pierre Mendès-France, the French Prime
Minister, was forced to resign. He was
replaced in 1959 by the French hero of the
Second World War, General Charles de
Gaulle. Even though de Gaulle held right-
wing opinions, not normally sympathetic to
terrorist campaigns, he straight away set
about negotiating a ceasefire with the FLN.
Can you suggest why?

The French army commander in Algeria,
General Salan, refused to obey de Gaulle's
orders. He joined the *pieds noirs* and formed
the Secret Army Organisation (OAS –
Organisation de l'Armée Sécrète), to attack both
the FLN and the French government.
There was further bloodshed, in Algeria
and in France. Algeria finally became
independent in 1962.

▲ **SOURCE 23**
French troops keep
watch over the
blanket-covered
body of a young
French Algerian
shot dead in the
street by a FLN
gunman.

QUESTIONS

1 *How did the following groups of people
feel about the situation in Algeria before
1954: pieds noirs; Algerians; people in
France?*

2 *What was the attitude towards
independence held by each group?*

3 *Why was the fighting so fierce on both
sides during the Algerian War?*

4 *Why do you think the French army
commander refused to accept de Gaulle's
plans for peace?*

5 *Why was the French experience of leaving
Algeria so different from the peaceful
handover achieved by Britain in some
other African states?*

Why did Kenya have to fight for independence?

The British colony of Kenya lasted less than one lifetime. Britain took over Kenya in 1888, white settlement only began after 1901 and independence came in 1963. Yet for a while many whites regarded Kenya as their dream colony, before that dream ended in a bloody and brutal war.

Between 1895 and 1901 the British built a 1,000 km railway from the coast through Kenya to Uganda, using Indian workers. The railway was expensive and the British government looked for ways of making some money by encouraging people to settle along the line. The only trouble was that they did not own the land. They therefore came up with the idea that settlers could move onto land which was 'vacant'. During the 1890s the local people, the Kikuyu, had been hit by disease, which had temporarily reduced their numbers. Much of their ancestral lands were therefore, at the time, not being used. White settlers moved in and loved it, especially in the 'White Highlands'.

In the 1920s the settlers did well, growing coffee, cotton and other cash crops for export. In 1922 they even tried to kidnap the governor to set up their own whites-only government, as in Rhodesia and South Africa. However, the white population was much smaller than in these countries or in Algeria (see page 107): only 9,000 whites and 4 million Africans. For the time being, however, the British government usually did what the settlers wanted, forcing Africans to work at low wages and forbidding African farmers from growing coffee.

Kenyan resistance

Protests by Africans started in the 1920s and quickened in the 1930s. Africans, particularly members of the largest group of people, the Kikuyu, began to run their own schools. There were only 40 such schools in 1912, but 2,000 by 1930. They also ran their own African Christian churches. Rising population brought further resentment as Africans found themselves excluded from lands which had been theirs. Many without

▲ **SOURCE 24**
Mau Mau suspects being identified by Kikuyu guards, 1953.

The Kikuyu came under the influence of Kenyatta, a demonic figure with extreme left-wing views. The driving force of the Mau Mau movement was ... the expulsion of the white man; its methods were the methods of African witchcraft. The Mau Mau oath is the most bestial, filthy and nauseating which perverted minds can ever have brewed. I can recall no instance when I have felt the forces of evil to be so near and so strong. As I wrote ... I would suddenly see a shadow fall across the page - the horned shadow of the Devil himself.

▲ **SOURCE 25**
From the memoirs of Oliver Lyttelton, British Colonial Secretary during the Mau Mau period, published in 1962.

land drifted to towns to find work. During the Second World War 97,000 Kenyans joined up to fight. The army gave them an education and they saw how the war had changed world attitudes to colonialism (see page 102). By 1945 Kenya, like much of Africa, was in a turbulent state.

Jomo Kenyatta

Jomo Kenyatta was born in 1894. He had been involved in resistance in the 1930s and had gone to London. He married a British wife, studied and visited Moscow. In 1946 he returned to Kenya and soon became the obvious leader of African opposition. By 1947 he was President of the Kenya African

Union. At the same time more impatient Kenyan nationalists were beginning a movement of violent protest against white rule. It was called Mau Mau (probably from the words 'uma uma' which mean 'out, out'). White settlers and Kikuyu who did not join Mau Mau were savagely killed and their cattle maimed. Oaths were sworn to encourage secrecy.

What was Kenyatta's attitude to Mau Mau? He shared their basic aims: to drive out foreigners and regain the lands which, they said, had been stolen by the settlers. There is no evidence that he approved of their violence which he denounced several times. Such distinctions were not made by the whites who demanded that he should be locked up. In 1953 he was tried and imprisoned.

The war against the Mau Mau between 1952 and 1960 was really a civil war (see Source 24). As in Vietnam (see page 130) villages were uprooted in order to keep them 'safe'. Some 10,000 Mau Mau, nearly 2,000 African civilians and 32 whites were killed. At first the British government seems to have taken the same attitude to Mau Mau and Kenyatta as the whites in Kenya (Source 25). By 1960 the war had cost the British taxpayer £55 million and it was clear that peace had to be made on the basis of power-sharing between whites and Africans. The more moderate white settlers could see that they could not continue whites-only rule and would have to do what the British government wanted. The British Prime Minister Harold Macmillan (see page 106) appointed Iain Macleod as Colonial Secretary. He organised a conference in London at Lancaster House in 1960 which proposed a new government with majority African rule.

Kenya was still very divided when Kenyatta was released from prison in 1961. Many whites felt totally hostile to black rule. Only the fall in the value of their farms prevented them from leaving. Africans who were not Kikuyu were anxious about their safety under the rule of the Kikuyu majority. Jomo Kenyatta showed great statesmanship in uniting the country. He appointed non-Kikuyu Africans to key posts and won over white settlers by his attitude (Source 27). After Kenya became independent in 1963 Kenyatta remained president of the country until his death in 1978.

◄ **SOURCE 26**
Jomo Kenyatta in 1960.

66

There is no society of angels, whether it is white, brown or black. We are all human beings and as such we are bound to make mistakes. If I have done a wrong to you, it is for you to forgive me; if you have done something wrong to me, it is for me to forgive you ... You have something to forget, just as I have.

99

▲ **SOURCE 27**
From a speech made by Jomo Kenyatta to white farmers in 1963.

QUESTIONS

1 Use these pages and page 102 to explain how nationalist feeling in Kenya grew in the years before 1945.

2 What did each of the following groups want in Kenya in 1945 and how did they intend to go about achieving their aims? White settlers; the British Government; Jomo Kenyatta; Mau Mau leadership.

3 What do you think were the key differences between the situation in Kenya and the situation in Algeria (see page 107)?

4 Who was to blame for the civil war in Kenya, 1952 – 1960?

Rebuilding Europe

In 1945, Europe was in ruins. Thirty million people had been killed. There were 25 million refugees and families without homes. In Germany alone, there were 15 million unemployed. Food, clothing and even paper were rationed. Many factories had been bombed; others had been converted to make weapons or planes, and were quite unsuited to manufacturing peacetime goods.

Almost worse than this, European nations felt a tremendous sense of shock. Their lands, unlike Britain, had been invaded and occupied. They had learned that desperate peoples, even the highly educated and 'civilised' Germans, could not be trusted. Their shattered continent seemed very small and vulnerable beside the superpower giants, the USA and USSR. How could Europe recover?

A united Europe?

The only answer was co-operation. Together, European nations could build stronger economies and, hopefully, a safer world. They could set up a huge 'common market', giving preference to European-made goods. If they worked alongside each other, no one nation could overrule the rest. Together, they could create a 'united states of Europe', to play a leading part in the post-war world.

Most important of all, as part of a united Europe, Germany might seem less of a threat. A rebuilt Europe would have to include Germany, but, understandably, many European countries who had only just been freed from the German invaders felt nervous about this. Yet no one wanted to repeat the mistakes made at the end of the First World War, when the harsh peace treaty terms and crushing REPARATIONS led to resentment among the German people. As a result, they had welcomed Hitler in the 1930s because he promised to solve their problems.

Building unity

How could European unity be achieved? There were two main issues involved: political agreement and economic co-operation. Both would be needed for a truly united Europe. In 1948, European leaders:

STEPS TO EUROPEAN UNITY

Date	Event
PHASE 1 – REBUILDING EUROPE	
1946	Winston Churchill calls for a 'United States of Europe'.
1947	Treaty of Dunkirk (Britain and France) aims at 'constant consultation' in economic matters and joint military action against attack.
1947	Marshall Plan: USA gives aid to war-damaged Europe.
1948	Treaty of Brussels: Benelux joins Dunkirk alliance.
1948	Organisation for European Economic Co-operation (OEEC) set up to re-build Europe. 16 nations join. Aims at co-operation in agriculture, fisheries, trade, transport, power supplies.
1948	European leaders meet at The Hague; discuss plans for a European Parliament. Council of Europe established (1949), but has few effective powers.
1949	NATO (North Atlantic Treaty Organisation) set up; multi-national, institutional co-operation: European nations (not Germany) plus USA against USSR.
1950	Plan for a European Defence Community; vetoed by Britain and, later, by France.
1950	Schuman Plan suggests France and West Germany work together to rebuild coal and steel industries; Britain (a major producer) refuses to join.
1951	Treaty of Paris: European Coal and Steel Community (ECSC) formed (France, West Germany, Italy, Benelux). Permanent ruling body (President: Jean Monnet), plus Court of Justice, Assembly and Secretariat; begins work in 1952. Policies to be community-wide, not decided by individual member nations.
1954	Western European Union formed (Britain, France, West Germany, Benelux); supervises re-armament of West Germany and its admission (1955) to NATO.
1955	Encouraged by the success of ECSC, a committee formed (Chairman: Paul-Henri Spaak of Belgium) to discuss further European economic co-operation.
1956	Spaak Committee recommends establishing European Economic Community.
1957	European Atomic Energy Community (EURATOM) formed (France, West Germany, Italy, Benelux). Aimed to encourage research, build reactors and share costs. As with ECSC, supra-national administration and decision-making bodies set up.
1957	TREATY OF ROME sets up EUROPEAN ECONOMIC COMMUNITY (EEC). Members: France, West Germany, Italy, Belgium, Netherlands, Luxembourg. Britain refuses to join.

Jean Monnet of France, Paul-Henri Spaak of Belgium, Alcide de Gasperi of Italy and Konrad Adenauer of West Germany, met to discuss how their nations might work together politically. As a result, they formed the Council of Europe.

But the real breakthrough came with a plan for economic collaboration in the coal and steel industries. This was drawn up in 1950 by the French politician Robert Schuman. The plan worked brilliantly:

STEPS TO EUROPEAN UNITY

Date	Event
PHASE 2 – WORKING TOGETHER	
1958	Common Agricultural Policy (CAP) planned (begins 1962).
1962	First meeting of European Parliament.
1965	ECSC, EURATOM and EEC amalgamate and become the EUROPEAN COMMUNITY (EC).
1967	Value Added Tax (VAT) introduced in all member states.
1968	European Customs Union formed – customs duties between members abolished to encourage inter-community trade.
1973	Britain, Ireland and Denmark join EC.
1973	EC signs treaties with two other international economic communities: GATT (General Agreement on Tariffs and Trade) and EFTA (European Free Trade Area).
1975	First Lomé Convention: regulates trade between Third World countries and EC.
1975	European Council formed (regular meetings between heads of member states to discuss EC policies on a wide range of topics, not just economics).
1975	European Regional Development Fund set up to give aid to poorer EC members.
1979	First direct elections to European Parliament.
1979	European Monetary System links member states' currencies.
1981	Greece joins EC.
1986	Spain and Portugal join EC.
1989	European Bank for Reconstruction and Development (EBRD) set up to help former communist states of Eastern Europe.
1990	East Germany and West Germany unite; 'United Germany' joins EC.
1991	Maastricht Summit proposes closer economic and political links between members. British government disagrees.
1992	Danish referendum rejects Maastricht agreement.
1993	Start of the Single European Market. In a second referendum, the Danes agree to the Maastricht proposals.

French and German industry made a rapid recovery. It also showed that it was possible for institutions involving two or more European states to work well, without causing major political problems.

The Council of Europe and the Schuman Plan for the European Coal and Steel Community (ECSC) were the key first steps towards a more comprehensive scheme aimed at European unity. There were many others. You can see them detailed in the time chart. After careful discussions of shared aims and ambitions (Source 28), the European Economic Community was established in 1957. It joined with Schuman's ECSC and EURATOM (European atomic power authority) to form the European Community in 1965. Britain did not become a member until 1973. Can you suggest reasons why?

Like it or loathe it?

Today, the European Community is run by an imposing administration and controls a vast budget (Source 29). It costs each European citizen about £99.50 per year. It regulates almost all aspects of European people's lives. There are community directives governing everything from the amount of sugar in jam to international computer systems. It controls the prices farmers receive for Europe's key foodstuffs (milk and wheat) and limits the number of foreign products (such as Japanese cars) sold in the European market. It has powers to control nuclear power, banking, immigration and television broadcasts. It sets standards for environmental protection. It has published plans that will lead to political and monetary union by 2000. It is admired, hated, respected and feared.

SOURCE 28

The aims of the European Community

- Ever closer union of the peoples of Europe.
- Improvement of living and working conditions through concerted action to guarantee steady expansion, balanced trade and fair competition.
- A reduction in economic differences between regions.
- Progressive abolition of restrictions on international trade.
- Aid for overseas development.
- Preservation and strengthening of peace and liberty.

SOURCE 29 ▶
Community income and expenditure.

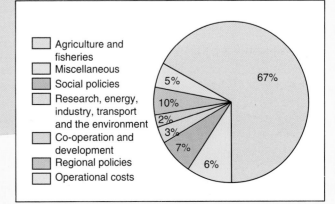

- Agriculture and fisheries
- Miscellaneous
- Social policies
- Research, energy, industry, transport and the environment
- Co-operation and development
- Regional policies
- Operational costs

67%
5%
10%
2%
3%
7%
6%

Britain in Europe?

How and why did attitudes in Britain towards the EEC gradually change?

The EEC (later known as the European Community) was founded in 1957. Yet Britain did not join until 1973. Why did Britain stay out of Europe for so long? Were British leaders hostile, uncertain or scared? Did their views match the feelings of ordinary men and women in the street?

In 1946, the British wartime leader Winston Churchill made the speech quoted in Source 30. Yet only five years later, in 1951, the Labour Prime Minister, Clement Attlee, refused to take part in discussions about the European Coal and Steel Community. This was not a party political matter: in 1952, Churchill, back in power as Conservative Prime Minister, also refused to join the ECSC. Was Britain 'turning its back' on Europe? If so, why?

European nations certainly thought that Britain was rejecting their plans. They felt angered by Britain's refusal to share their enthusiasm for a new, united, Europe. They accused Britain, with some justification, of preferring an American alliance.

As Source 31 reveals, in 1957, when the European Economic Community was being formed, Britain believed that European co-operation would not work. British politicians, and many ordinary people, also feared that joining the EEC would mean giving up 'sovereignty' or the right of a country to manage its own affairs. They did not want to be ruled from Brussels by people they called 'faceless BUREAUCRATS'. Joining the EEC meant betraying Britain's proudly independent past.

Trade unions thought that jobs might be lost if industry was reorganised on a European-wide basis. They also saw the EEC as a 'bosses club', where union rights would not be respected. Farmers and other workers in Britain's Celtic fringes (Scotland, Wales and Northern Ireland) feared that the centralised European administration would be out of touch with their needs.

Britain's economic policy-makers also favoured staying out of Europe. In the

SOURCE 30

If Europe is to be saved from infinite misery, and indeed from final doom, there must be an act of faith in the European family. ... We must build a kind of United States of Europe.

(Comment by Winston Churchill, 1946.)

SOURCE 31

Gentlemen, I have listened to your discussions with interest and sympathy. I must tell you that this future treaty you have been asked to prepare is not likely to be concluded; should it be concluded, it's not likely to be ratified; should it be ratified, it's even less likely to be applied.

(Comment by British government official at talks before the Treaty of Rome, 1957.)

1950s, they believed that EEC membership would damage existing trading links with Commonwealth countries, especially Australia and New Zealand, which provided large amounts of cheap food for Britain to import. They calculated that the Common Agricultural Policy would lead to higher food prices in Britain, and cause problems for British farmers. And so, in 1959, instead of joining the EEC, Britain allied with other non-EEC countries to form the European Free Trade Area. The government hoped that this would provide a larger market for British and Commonwealth goods.

A change of mind

British governments gradually came to change their policies towards Europe. This was partly because of the personal beliefs of two Conservative leaders, Harold Macmillan and Edward Heath. It was also because contact with the expanding European economy brought changes in the types of goods ordinary British people wanted to buy. French wines and cheeses, Italian fruit, German machinery and cars, all impressed British consumers by their attractiveness and high quality. By joining the EEC, British manufacturers hoped to share in Europe's success. Deals made with Commonwealth countries still accounted for half Britain's international trade, but between 1959 and 1964 British trade with Europe almost doubled, while its trade with the Commonwealth rose by only 2 per cent.

'Oui' or 'Non'?

Britain applied to join the EEC in 1961. But at the same time, it also demanded major changes in the way the Community was run. You can see how one British cartoonist portrayed this in Source 32. Existing

▲ SOURCE 32
Cartoon in a British newspaper, 1961, showing three European leaders (left to right): De Gaulle (France), Adenauer (West Germany) and Macmillan (Britain).

Carry out a survey of attitudes to Europe and the EC. Work out a short questionnaire of three or four questions with 'yes/no' answers. For example: 'Do you think the EC intervenes too much in our lives? Is their intervention good or bad for most people?'

Interview as many people as you can. Note their age and sex. Put your results in a table. What conclusions can you draw? Does age or sex make any difference?

Look out for similar polls in the newspapers or TV and compare your own results with theirs.

Commonwealth and EFTA trade links were to be protected, and the Common Agricultural Policy was to be revised to suit British farmers, who worked in a different way from their European 'peasant' counterparts. Not surprisingly, when faced with all these demands, the French President, de Gaulle, said *'Non'*.

Britain re-applied for membership in 1967. Even though, this time, Britain made fewer demands for changes to Community policies, de Gaulle still refused to accept the application. Other European countries were unhappy about this, but were powerless to overturn the French VETO.

De Gaulle retired in 1969, but British politicians now faced increasing opposition at home. People were calling for a referendum to decide whether Britain should join Europe, something that had not been held in Britain before. Edward Heath, who was now Conservative Prime Minister, ignored these protests, and negotiated Britain's entry into the EC in 1973.

When, in 1975, the new Labour government did hold a referendum (as they had promised to do before the general election that returned them to power), the results showed that over two-thirds of British voters supported Heath's decision. Britain had joined Europe at last.

Review

Common Market or Commonwealth?

Look back at page 97. Why has the Commonwealth not proved to be a world power despite 50 member countries comprising a quarter of the world's population? Why is the European Community more important to Britain?

1 **Target Questions**

1 **What different attitudes towards European economic co-operation could be found in Britain between 1946 and 1975?**

2 **Why were there such differences?**

3 **Why did the European policies of British governments change between 1951 and 1973?**

4 **How did people in different jobs feel about the European Community?**

5 **Did all politicans share the same views?**

Conflict and

In this unit you will find out about the superpowers, the USA and the USSR, and the conflict between them, called the Cold War. We shall also see how the United Nations has tried to preserve peace and how, in recent years, the superpowers have begun to co-operate.

We shall end by looking at the state of the world at the end of this century.

Key Questions

What is the Cold War and how did it begin?

How close did the superpowers come to war?

How has the UN changed since 1945 and how successsful has it been?

How did the Cold War end?

Why was Europe a Cold War battleground?

What was the impact of the Cold War on other parts of the world?

Every year since 1945 there has been a war going on somewhere in the world. Civil wars, religious wars, racial wars, wars of conquest or defence. What has that got to do with us?

The answer lies in Source 1. Throughout the period from 1945 to 1990 the two great world superpowers, the USA and the USSR, were in conflict with each other. It never came to actual war between them but there was always the fear that it would. Both superpowers had nuclear weapons, like the one shown being tested in Source 1.

The only nuclear weapons ever to be used in war were the two dropped on Hiroshima and Nagasaki in Japan in 1945. The one on Hiroshima killed 75,000 people at once and 100,000 more died afterwards.

co-operation

◄ **SOURCE 1**
Nuclear test explosion at Bikini Atoll in the Pacific Ocean, 1956.

◄ **SOURCE 3**
A UN Food and Agriculture Organisation helicopter used for spraying locusts in West Africa.

▲ **SOURCE 2**
United Nations aid convoy taking food to victims of war, Yugoslavia 1993.

Since 1945 much bigger bombs have been made and tested. Their destructive power is enormous. A 1-megaton bomb has these effects:

- Blast. Houses up to 7km away totally destroyed.
- Heat. People close to the explosion totally vaporised, people severely burnt up to 10km away. Houses catch fire up to 8km away.

- Radiation. Radioactive fallout can spread for hundreds of kilometres downwind, causing sickness, sterility, malformation in babies and death.

Some scientists think that if a nuclear war took place, with several nuclear explosions, the dust would blot out the sun. This idea is called the nuclear winter. The temperature of the earth would fall, crops would fail and most people, possibly all life on earth, would come to an end.

Co-operation
Alongside these new and terrible destructive forces, people also work for peace. The main international organisation which works for peace is the United Nations. There are two sides to peacemaking. One is stopping war, or helping those who are suffering from war (see Source 2). The other is trying to remove the causes of war, by helping people lead healthy, satisfied lives (see Source 3).

The superpowers and the Cold War

What is a superpower?

The Second World War left the old European 'Great Powers' of Britain, France and Germany exhausted and in chaos. Two nations stood out clearly above all the others, the USA and the USSR. So great was their military and economic power that their influence was world-wide: they were now superpowers. Both of these countries had some similar features.

- They were both large countries: the USA covered 9 million sq km, the USSR 21 million sq km.
- They both had large populations: USA 226 million, USSR 262 million (1984).
- They both had large armies: USA 2 million personnel, USSR 4.8 million (1984). After 1949 they both had nuclear weapons – see Source 5.
- They were both rich: USA $2,100 billion, USSR $1,200 billion (GNP 1984).

IDEOLOGICAL DIFFERENCES

USA: Capitalism	USSR: Communism
Business and industry owned by private individuals.	Business and industry owned by the state.
Employers run their business as they choose. They hire or fire workers, open or shut factories.	State runs all businesses, fixes wages and prices.
They may go bankrupt or make big profits.	State provides jobs, housing, education and health services for everyone.
Workers' wages fixed with employer.	Workers are guaranteed a job but have to work where the state sends them.
Workers can change jobs.	No great wealth or poverty.
Great differences in wealth and poverty.	Democracy means voting for the candidate of the only permitted party, the Communist Party.
Democracy means two or more parties and free elections.	

▼ **SOURCE 4**
Parade of USSR's nuclear missiles in Moscow, 1985.

You can read about the origins of the Cold War on page 120, but one major cause was the IDEOLOGICAL differences between them. They had very different ideas about how a country, and other countries should be run (see box above).

National interests

Some people have argued that it was not ideologies that separated the superpowers. They were simply two powerful nations trying to look after their own interests and so coming into conflict. The USSR felt the need for security. It had been invaded in 1914 and again in 1941. Over 20 million of its citizens had died during the Second World War. It wanted to be safe.

The USA was secure, but needed to trade with the rest of the world to support its own high standard of living. Between the two world wars, the USA had had a policy of isolationism: not getting involved in affairs outside America. Many Americans felt that this had been wrong. It had allowed dictators to flourish and had helped lead eventually to the Second World War. They now wanted to use the power of the USA to play a major role in the world. The USA was encouraged in this by its allies, especially those in Western Europe who felt threatened by the USSR's search for security.

What is a Cold War?

A Cold War is waging war against an enemy country by every means short of actually fighting. After the USSR tested its first atom bomb in 1949, both sides were involved in an arms race (see Sources 4 and 5) with each side trying to make the most weapons. By the 1960s both had enough nuclear warheads to destroy each other many times over. This was called 'Mutually Assured Destruction' (MAD). In theory it meant that neither side dared to go to war, because its own country would be destroyed as well. This was a risky way of keeping the peace, as each side developed new methods of nuclear attack and defence, trying to get ahead of the other.

Each side spied on the other, trying to find out their plans. Source 6 shows a U2 US spy-plane. This could fly at a great height, too high for Soviet fighters to shoot it down. It took photographs of Soviet military installations. A photograph taken by a U2 can be seen in Source 32 on page 128.

Each side made alliances with other countries. The result was that most of the countries in the world were part of one or the other power blocs. If a war broke out, the USA and the USSR supported opposite sides, often supplying them with weapons.

Time chart

1945	End of Second World War
1947	Marshall Plan. Truman Doctrine
1948–1949	Berlin blockade and airlift
1949	NATO. USSR tests atom bomb
1950–1953	Korean War
1955	Warsaw Pact
1956	Hungarian revolt
1961	Berlin Wall built, US involved in Vietnam
1962	Cuban Missile Crisis
1968	Non-Proliferation Treaty. Czechoslovakia revolts
1972	SALT – 1
1979	SALT – 2
1983	Cruise missiles in Europe
1987	INF Treaty
1989	Berlin Wall destroyed.

▼ SOURCE 5
The arms race: nuclear warheads of the USA and USSR, 1967 to 1981.

SOURCE 6 ▶
A U2 spy-plane.

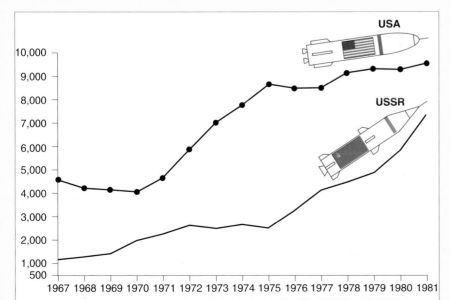

QUESTIONS

1 It can be said that under capitalism the individual person is more important than the state, under communism the state is more important than the individual. Use the table of differences between capitalism and communism to explain what this means.

2 What are the benefits and disadvantages of each system?

3 Which system do you think is best at running business and industry successfully?

The United Nations

Why was the United Nations set up?

Your school has rules. If you break them there are punishments. These are called 'sanctions'. You obey the school rules partly because they are sensible and partly because you do not want to be punished. Our country has laws. If you break them you are fined or sent to prison. We have a police force, courts and prisons to enforce the law.

But what about nations which do wrong? What laws are broken if one country attacks another? Who makes these laws, who enforces them? What sanctions can be used?

After the First World War the nations of the world decided there had to be a better way of solving disputes than going to war. They set up the League of Nations. Even though it failed to stop the Second World War, the Allies were keen to try again.

In the middle of the Second World War, the 'Big Four' of the USA, USSR, Britain and China, met in Moscow in 1943 and agreed on a plan to set up a general international organisation. This body would be based on the principle of the 'sovereign equality of all peace-loving states' and membership would be open to all such states, large or small, in order to keep international peace and security.

A year later, in 1944, representatives of the 'Big Four' met at Dumbarton Oaks in the USA to work out details of how the new organisation would operate.

▲ **SOURCE 7**
The United Nations headquarters in New York.

▼ **SOURCE 8**
Cartoon, 1950, comparing the UN with the League of Nations.

In 1945 the leaders of 50 nations met at San Francisco to draw up the UN Charter. The first meeting of the General Assembly of 51 member states was held in London in 1946. The United Nations (UN) had come into being.

The UN and the League of Nations

The founders of the UN wanted to learn the lessons of the failure of the League of Nations to keep the peace in the years between the First and Second World Wars (Source 8). They therefore made some key differences:
- Every nation should belong. (Several important states were not members of the League for all or part of its existence.)
- The Security Council should meet regularly and be able to respond rapidly. (The Council of the League only met occasionally.)
- The Secretary-General should play a large part and take decisive personal action. (The League had no such job.)
- The UN should be able to use force. This has become the most controversial of the powers of the UN, as some states argue that force has not been used impartially. UN forces are not allowed to interfere in the internal affairs of a country.

◄ **SOURCE 9**
The General Assembly in session.

SECURITY COUNCIL

Five permanent members: USA, USSR, China, Britain and France, plus ten other countries, in turn. The five permanent members each have a veto: that is, they can block the Security Council from acting. This reflects the fact that the UN was set up by the great powers, but it also reflects the realities of world politics. The Security Council can meet quickly to deal with a crisis. They can: offer arbitration in a disagreement between states; impose economic sanctions, such as a trade boycott on a state which is acting wrongly; call upon troops from member nations to use force to end a war.

INTERNATIONAL COURT OF JUSTICE

The 15 international judges hear cases in disputes between countries.

GENERAL ASSEMBLY

One country, one vote. Meets in New York. All other parts of the UN are responsible to the General Assembly.

SECRETARY GENERAL

The six Secretary-Generals of the UN have been: Trygve Lie (Norway) 1946–53; Dag Hammarskjöld (Sweden) 1953–61; U Thant (Burma) 1961–71; Kurt Waldheim (Austria) 1971–81, Pérez de Cuellar (Peru) 1981–91; Boutros Boutros Ghali (Egypt) from 1991.

SOCIAL AND ECONOMIC COUNCIL

Co-ordinates the work of the UN agencies.

UN AGENCIES

  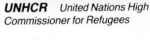

WHO *World Health Organisation*
Runs education programmes on hygiene, family planning and health care. Has eliminated smallpox, but not malaria, bilharzia or dysentry.

FAO *Food and Agriculture Organisation*
Brings food aid in famines, but also teaches people better farming methods.

UNICEF *United Nations International Children's Emergency Fund*
Helps children with food and education.

UNESCO *United Nations Educational Scientific and Cultural Organisation*
Deals with education and tries to bring people of different nations to better understanding of each other.

UNHCR *United Nations High Commissioner for Refugees*

UNCTAD *United Nations Conference on Trade and Development*
Tries – with not much success – to improve trading conditions for poorer nations.

ILO *International Labour Organisation*
Deals with working conditions.

IMF *International Monetary Fund*
Deals with governments' immediate financial problems.

World Bank
Provides long-term loans for countries.

Nevertheless, armed forces wearing the pale blue UN berets have been used in Greece, Indonesia, Palestine, Egypt, Lebanon, Korea (see pages 124 and 125), Kashmir, Congo/Zaire (see page 135), North Yemen, Cyprus, Dominican Republic, Cambodia, Kuwait and the former Yugoslavia (see page 115).

While the lack of effective sanctions has hampered the UN's efforts to bring peace, the agencies of the UN (see box) have worked to eliminate the causes of war: poverty, ignorance and disease.

QUESTIONS

▲ The United Nations Organisation

1　*Do you think it is fair that the five permanent members of the Security Council should have a veto? What problems could arise?*

2　*Why do you think the UN is not allowed to intervene in the internal affairs of member countries? What should they do in a civil war?*

How did the Cold War begin?

Look at Source 10. As Hitler's resistance crumbles away, victorious soldiers meet in Germany: Americans from the west, Russians from the east. They are friendly allies. Yet within a year the battle lines for the Cold War had been drawn up. Cold War attitudes had been formed which were to last for the next 40 years. How could this happen?

Yalta and Potsdam

When Stalin (USSR), Roosevelt (USA) and Churchill (Britain) met at Yalta in February 1945 they agreed on the division of Germany after the war (see page 122). Stalin also got the Allies to agree that the borders of the USSR should be moved westwards at the expense of Poland. He suggested that Poland should be compensated by taking land from Eastern Germany (see Source 11).

Roosevelt and Churchill were not happy about this, but they needed to keep the wartime alliance alive. There was little they could do about it as the Red Army already occupied all the areas in question. They

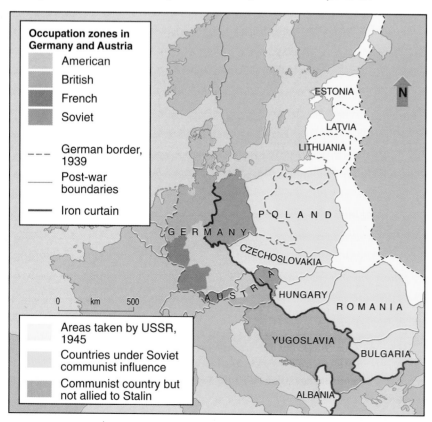

▲ **SOURCE 10**
US and Red Army soldiers meet in Germany, May 1945.

▼ **SOURCE 11**
Map of Eastern Europe 1945.

Occupation zones in Germany and Austria
- American
- British
- French
- Soviet

- – – German border, 1939
- —— Post-war boundaries
- —— Iron curtain

- Areas taken by USSR, 1945
- Countries under Soviet communist influence
- Communist country but not allied to Stalin

ESTONIA
LATVIA
LITHUANIA
POLAND
GERMANY
CZECHOSLOVAKIA
AUSTRIA
HUNGARY
ROMANIA
YUGOSLAVIA
BULGARIA
ALBANIA

0   km   500

N

persuaded Stalin to agree to hold free elections in Poland.

By the time of the Potsdam Conference in July 1945, things were different. Roosevelt had died, and had been replaced by his vice-president, Harry Truman. Churchill lost the British general election during the conference and was replaced by the Labour Party leader, Clement Attlee. Stalin meanwhile had set up a communist, pro-Soviet government in Poland and arrested several non-communist Poles. The same thing seemed to be about to happen in Czechoslovakia and Hungary. Truman was furious. There were misunderstandings on both sides.

The American view

This was particularly put forward by Truman's adviser, Dean Acheson. He said that the Russians had set up governments in Eastern Europe that were not freely elected. The boundaries of the USSR had moved 450 km westwards, taking over 22 million more people. Countries in chaos after the war were easy prey to communist takeover. The communists would soon be in control of Western Europe if they weren't stopped.

The Russian view

The Russians said that they had been attacked through Poland in 1914, 1920 and 1941. They wanted a friendly government in Poland and elsewhere in Eastern Europe in order to protect themselves. The USA had the atom bomb and were trying to control the world.

SOURCE 12

Y̲ou evidently don't agree that the Soviet Union is entitled to seek in Poland a government that would be friendly to it. To put it plainly: you want us to set aside the security of the Soviet Union, but I cannot proceed against the interest of my own country.

(Stalin wrote this to US President Truman in 1946.)

SOURCE 14

The real peace treaty we need now is between the USA and Russia. There will always be ideological conflict, but that is no reason why diplomats cannot work out a basis for both systems to live safely in the world side by side.

(Henry Wallace criticises Truman's attitude, September 1946.)

SOURCE 13

From the Baltic to the Adriatic an Iron Curtain has descended across the continent.

(From Winston Churchill's speech at Fulton, Missouri, USA, in March 1946.)

SOURCE 15

A̲t the present moment nearly every nation must choose between alternative ways of life. The choice is too often not a free one. One way of life is based on the will of the majority, free elections, freedom of speech and freedom from political oppression.

The second way of life is based on the will of a minority forcibly imposed on the majority. It relies on terror and oppression, a controlled press and radio, fixed elections.

I believe that it must be the policy of the USA to support free peoples who are resisting attempted subjugation by armed minorities and outside pressure.

(The Truman Doctrine: President Truman's speech, March 1947.)

The Truman Doctrine

Hostility increased on both sides. Soon movement between Eastern and Western Europe was impossible. Both the USA and USSR began to increase spending on weapons. Winston Churchill, in a speech in the USA, described the 'Iron Curtain' that had fallen across Europe (see Sources 11 and 13).

Opinion in the USA was not united at first. Henry Wallace, who had also been one of Truman's advisers, felt that the USA and USSR should live and let live (Source 14).

Matters came to a head in 1947. There was a civil war in Greece between royalists and communists. Britain was helping the royalists, but could not afford to do so any longer and suggested that the USA should help. The USA was not really interested in Greece, but Truman decided that he could not let the communists take over another country. He spoke to the US Congress (Source 15), persuading them to grant aid to the anti-communist forces worth US$400 million.

The last paragraph of Source 15 was later known as 'the Truman Doctrine'. This policy was called 'containment': an effort to contain communism, in order to stop it spreading anywhere else. It was to be a huge commitment for the future.

1 Target Questions

1 *Explain how each of these things helped to bring about Cold War attitudes: the atom bomb; capitalism and communism; Polish elections; the conquest of Germany; the civil war in Greece.*

2 *Look at Sources 11, 12, 14 and 15. What would be the attitudes of: Stalin, Wallace and Truman, to the boundary changes shown in Source 11?*

3 *Why did Stalin and Truman hold the views they did?*

4 *What different views were held by the three Americans: Acheson, Truman and Wallace?*

Why did Berlin become a flashpoint?

In February 1945, Stalin, Roosevelt and Churchill met at Yalta in the USSR. Their main aim was to decide how Germany was to be dealt with as the war ended. They were not in generous mood. Wider public knowledge of the Holocaust had brought anger on all sides.

Stalin wanted Germany to pay $20 billion in reparation; half of this would go to the USSR to rebuild the terrible losses they had sustained in the war. The three leaders agreed to divide Germany into occupation zones, one for each of the Allies. The city of Berlin, inside the Russian zone, should also be divided. The French were give the same powers later in 1945, making four zones (see Source 16).

Conditions inside Germany in 1945 and 1946 were terrible. Cities had been destroyed; there were food shortages (see Source 17) and shortages of medical supplies; there was no proper currency so people bartered or used cigarettes as currency. The population was swollen by 16 million refugees expelled from Eastern Europe. Britain and France were in no position to give food and money as their own economies were in great difficulties (see unit 2, page 48).

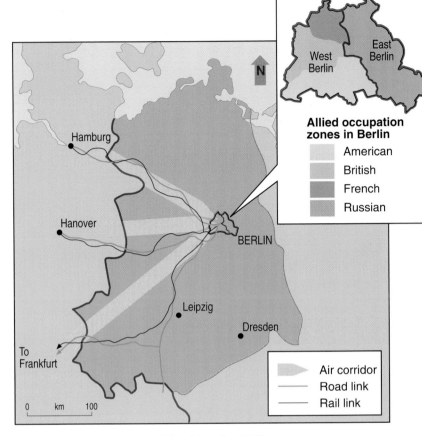

Allied occupation zones in Berlin

- American
- British
- French
- Russian

Air corridor

Road link

Rail link

▲ **SOURCE 16**
Germany and Berlin in 1945.

▼ **SOURCE 18**
Poster celebrating the Marshall Plan.

◄ **SOURCE 17**
German children clamber on a refuse heap looking for food, 1945.

The Marshall Plan

The US President, Harry Truman, felt that communism did well when people were desperate and their countries in ruins. He sent his Secretary of State, General George Marshall, to see how much European countries would need. Marshall told him $17 billion. The US Congress was not keen on the idea, but just as they were discussing it the news came of the brutal communist takeover of Czechoslovakia (see page 127). In June 1947 they agreed to grant $4 billion in immediate aid.

This 'Marshall Aid' was welcomed in Western Europe (Source 18). Overall, between 1948 and 1952, the USA gave $13 billion to Europe. Britain received the most: $3.1 billion (see Source 57 on page 49 for the effects). France received $2.7 billion and Germany $1.4 billion.

The Soviet Union was offered Marshall Aid, but Stalin refused it. He also stopped any Eastern European country from receiving it. He felt that the plan was just a way of extending US influence and dependence. Two different views are given in Source 19.

SOURCE 19

Two views of the Marshall Plan, from Truman (A), and the Russians (B).

A

The Marshall Plan will go down in history as one of America's greatest contributions to the peace of the world... without it, it would have been difficult for Western Europe to remain free of communism.

B

The plan was aimed at uniting countries on an anti-Soviet basis... a new alliance against communism.

Think about...

How much is this country influenced by the USA? How do you feel about this?

Both statements in Source 19 are probably sincere. How would each one reply to the other?

The Berlin blockade

It was clear to the Allies that if Western Europe was to stage an economic recovery it would have to include Germany. For several decades the economies of Western Europe had been interdependent. It was also clear that, for the sake of ordinary Germans, their country could not be left in ruins for ever. As a first step, the Allies proposed a new currency to be introduced in the Western zones in 1948.

Stalin was furious. His hatred of Germany was still strong. The problems of its starving people did not move him. He accused the West of rebuilding a Nazi state, and decided to put pressure on them.

Berlin was the place where the pressure was applied. The Russians began to make it difficult for supplies to get through from the Allied zones by road, rail or canal. By June 1948 it was a complete blockade.

What were the Allies to do? Here was a city of 2.1 million people. They needed 4,000 tons of food and other supplies per day. Should US troops fight their way in across the Soviet zone? Should they threaten to bomb Russia?

The airlift

The Allies took the least aggressive alternative. They decided to fly in supplies along three routes (see Sources 16 and 20). Plane after plane brought in supplies, 27,000 trips in all, from June 1948 to May 1949. It was an amazing achievement of organisation and technology.

> ## SOURCE 20
>
> The planes streamed across the sky, a glittering conveyor belt of aircraft. Most planes were piled to the hatches with coal but others carried every conceivable item a blockaded city would use: cocoa, sausages, oats, tobacco, manhole covers, dried banana flakes for sick children, 2,000 rubber hot water bottles for Berlin's hospitals, dried apricots and noodles.
>
> (The Berlin airlift, by Frank Donovan, who took part in it.)

Cold War not Hot War

The Allies avoided the warlike option by choosing to operate an airlift. The Russians also kept cool. They did not attempt to shoot down any planes. The Berlin blockade stayed part of the Cold War and not the beginning of World War Three.

NATO

German unity was now impossible. The three Allied zones, including West Berlin, joined to become West Germany, with the capital at Bonn. In 1949, the Western European countries joined an alliance with the USA: the North Atlantic Treaty Organisation (NATO). They agreed to defend one another if attacked. Western European leaders felt safer to have the might of the USA behind them. The British Foreign Minister said it brought 'a feeling of relief'.

Why did Korea become a flashpoint?

The US government thought 1949 was a bad year for them. First, the USSR tested its own atom bomb. The USA no longer had the advantage and conflict could be much more dangerous. Then the 23-year-long civil war in China ended with a communist victory. The US government saw this as another success in the communists' attempt to take over the world.

How should the US react? Did the Truman Doctrine (see page 121), worked out for Europe, apply to Asia? In 1949 the USA passed the National Security Act, setting up a National Security Council (NSC) to advise the president. In 1950 Truman's NSC sent him a document called NSC 68. This advised him that the US should oppose communism everywhere in the world. Truman did not have to wait long before putting this advice into action.

Korea

Korea had been divided since 1945 into a communist North Korea and a capitalist South Korea. In 1950 war broke out between them. It had three phases, as shown in Source 21.

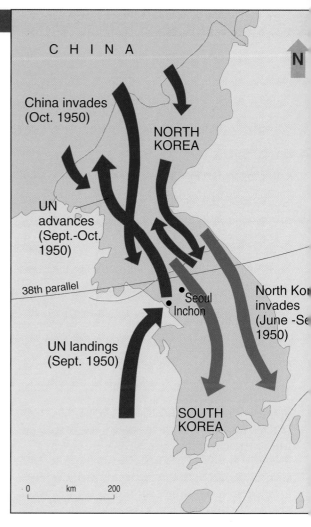

▲ **SOURCE 21**
The three main phases of the Korean war.

Phase 1 June to September 1950. North Korean troops invade South Korea. They soon occupied all of it except the south-east corner. They were probably acting on Stalin's advice.

Truman acted fast. By 1 July, US troops were helping the South Koreans. Truman also called on the UN to condemn the invasion, pointing to similarities with the Japanese invasion of Manchuria in 1931, and the Italian invasion of Ethiopia in 1935. The failure of the League of Nations on these occasions was seen as part of the drift to war in 1939. The USSR might have used its veto in the Security Council to block any UN action. At that time, however, the USSR was BOYCOTTING the UN because the UN refused to allow communist China to join. The Security Council was therefore able to back the use of force against North Korea.

◀ **SOURCE 22**
US forces land at Inchon, Korea, September 1950.

Phase 2 September to October 1950. US forces, together with others, under the UN flag, land at Inchon under the command of US General MacArthur (Source 22). MacArthur soon drove the North Korean forces out of South Korea, but then invaded North Korea, nearly reaching the Chinese border. This was a UN action, and 15 other nations took part, including Britain. (It was the cost of British rearmament for the Korean War that led to prescription charges being introduced, see page 61). In fact, however, the US provided 50 per cent of the army, 86 per cent of the navy and 93 per cent of the air force.

Phase 3 November 1950 to June 1953. The Chinese were alarmed at the US/UN advance and called on them to halt. MacArthur refused. A Chinese army of 300,000 then advanced south, driving all before it. MacArthur wanted to escalate the war by invading China. His reasons are given in Source 23, and he had a lot of support in the USA. Truman kept his cool and sacked MacArthur (Source 24). US policy was to be containment, not liberation. A ceasefire was agreed in November 1951, but peace was not made until 1953.

The results of the war
The Korean people suffered up to 3 million civilian casualties (see Source 25). For the two superpowers, the Cold War had clearly become world-wide. The USSR and USA became locked in an arms race, costing huge amounts of money.

In the next few years, under US Secretary of State John Foster Dulles, the US made world-wide alliances to parallel NATO. The South-East Asia Treaty Organisation (SEATO) of 1954 linked the US with Thailand, the Philippines and Pakistan. In the Baghdad Pact of 1955 the US joined Turkey, Iran, Iraq and Pakistan. (In 1959 Iraq left and it was renamed the Central Treaty Organisation – CENTO.)

The Russian response was to form its own military alliance in 1955 with all its own friends, called the Warsaw Pact.

▲ **SOURCE 25**
A Korean girl carries her wounded brother away from the fighting. It is estimated that about 3 million civilians from both countries died in the Korean War.

SOURCE 23

It seems strangely difficult for some to realise that here in Asia is where the communist conspirators have elected to make their play for global conquest. If we lose the war to communism in Asia, the fall of Europe is inevitable. There is no substitute for victory.

(US General MacArthur.)

SOURCE 24

Against the advantage of spreading the war to the mainland of China, there must be the risk of Russian intervention and of World War III.

(US President Truman.)

QUESTIONS

1 *What did MacArthur want the US to do? See Source 23.*

2 *Why did Truman disagree? See Source 24.*

3 *What does this disagreement tell us about US policies during the Cold War?*

4 *Who do you think were the winners and losers in the Korean War?*

What was life like behind the Iron Curtain?

What did it mean to be part of the Soviet bloc? How did people there react to the situation?

Although the USSR was large and powerful, the USA was richer. The USSR was not so efficient at wealth-producing as the USA, and the cost of the arms race had a serious impact on the Russian people's way of life. This was pointed out by Nikita Khrushchev, the Russian leader from 1955 to 1964 (Source 26).

Stalin had died in 1953. Khrushchev emerged as leader after two years of uncertainty. He said he wanted 'peaceful co-existence' with the West and competition in trade and ideas, not weapons. This would allow Russia to put more effort into improving the lives of Russian people.

In 1956, at the 20th Communist Party Congress, Khrushchev told some of the truth about Stalin. He spoke about Stalin's dictatorship and the way he had killed or removed his rivals. In the countries of Eastern Europe which Stalin had taken over after the war, this speech was taken to mean that things were going to change. There were demonstrations in Poland and East Berlin.

SOURCE 26

We must help people eat well, dress well and live well. You cannot put theory in your soup.... If after 40 years of communism a person cannot have a glass of milk or a pair of shoes he will not believe communism is a good idea, whatever you tell him.

(Khrushchev's description of the problems of the USSR.)

SOURCE 27

"Since early morning Russian troops have been attacking Budapest and our people. Please tell the world of the treacherous attack on our struggle for liberty. Help! Help! Help!

(Last broadcast of a Hungarian radio station, 5 November 1956.)"

Hungary

The Hungarians' experience of life behind the Iron Curtain was, in many ways, typical. The government did what Moscow told it to do. The Hungarian economy was tied into that of the Soviet Union, ignoring the country's own needs.

Hungary's standard of living actually fell by 5 per cent from 1949 to 1955. There were secret police everywhere, arresting people for criticising the government. There was no contact with the West. Western fashions were not available and Western pop music was banned.

Following Khrushchev's speech there were riots and symbols of Russian rule were attacked (see Source 28). A new government was formed which included non-communists. They discussed leaving the Warsaw Pact.

This was too much for Khrushchev. He sent in tanks to crush the revolt and some 30,000 people were killed. 'Peaceful co-existence' obviously did not mean endangering Russia by letting go of the countries Stalin had taken. The Hungarians appealed to the West (Source 27), but no help was sent. Once again Western leaders did not want to turn the Cold War into a 'Hot War'.

Berlin Wall, 1961

The contrast between the economic success of West Germany (including West Berlin) and the drab, backward East Germany was obvious. As a result, some 2 million East Germans fled to the West. In 1961, Khrushchev ordered the building of a wall right round the city, in order to stop this drain of citizens (Source 29). It lasted for 28 years before it was pulled down.

▼ **SOURCE 28**
Statue of Stalin being destroyed, Hungary 1956.

SOURCE 31

The new economic reforms can now go ahead without being blocked by the old hard-line communists. Czechoslovakia has finally taken a decision to pull its economic system into some kind of order – the kind of order that made it so successful before the war – and so it has had to rally support from the people. This can only be done by extending freedom and democracy.

(BBC report on events in Czechoslovakia, March 1968.)

Czechoslovakia, 1968

Between the wars Czechoslovakia had been a democratic and prosperous country. After 1948, communists loyal to Moscow had taken complete control. By the 1960s the economy was stagnant. There were few goods for sale and managers were appointed for their party loyalty rather than their abilities. There was no free speech and heavy censorship.

In 1967 Otto Sik, an economist, proposed changes. To be more efficient, the economy had to be more free. This would mean a more democratic approach in politics too.

In January 1968, Alexander Dubček was elected to the party leadership and the old pro-Moscow leaders left. Source 31 explains what was going on. Dubček allowed free discussion in the press, radio and television. People's rights to meet and talk freely were extended. Factories were to be run by boards of management which would include workers. All this was called the 'Prague Spring'.

Dubček tried to learn the lessons of Hungary in 1956. He did not want to leave the Warsaw Pact. He was a communist, but wanted 'communism with a human face'. However, the Russian leaders put him under tremendous pressure to resign. He refused, and in August they sent tanks in to remove him. The Czech people resisted them passively for several days (see Source 30), but in the end pro-Soviet rule was re-imposed.

---

1 *Target Questions*

1 *Choose two of the reasons below and explain how they caused the Czech revolt of 1968.*

- *Control from Moscow*
- *Press censorship*
- *Economic decline*
- *Otto Sik's plans*
- *Dubček's leadership*
- *Long tradition of independence*

2 *Do you agree that control from Moscow was the most important?*

3 *Explain how Dubček's leadership was both a result of the problems of Czechoslovakia and a cause of the revolt.*

4 *What other factors are involved in trying to write a full account of the causes of these events?*

 SOURCE 29
The Berlin Wall.

◄ **SOURCE 30**
Czech students trying to argue with Russian tank crews, Prague 1968.

Going to the brink: Cuba 1962

Who was to blame for taking the world to the brink of nuclear war over Cuba in 1962? Who pulled back from war? Who 'won'?

One of the areas where the USA and USSR were rivals was space exploration. The Russians scored a tremendous success in 1957 when they put a satellite, a 'sputnik', into orbit around the Earth. In 1962, a Russian, Yuri Gagarin, became the first person in space.

This space race was not all pure science. Space rockets which carried people could also carry nuclear missiles. It would be almost impossible to shoot them down. By 1962, the USA had nuclear missiles with a range of 1,000km based in Turkey, a NATO ally. These threatened several Russian cities, while even the longest-range Russian missiles (2,500km) could not reach American cities.

The Cuban Revolution

In 1959 Khrushchev was handed an opportunity to correct the balance. That year there was a revolution in Cuba: the pro-American government was overthrown by Fidel Castro. Castro began taking over land and wealth belonging to Americans. When the USA refused to buy Cuba's sugar crop, Castro sold it to the Russians. In 1961, anti-Castro Cubans, with some US help, landed in Cuba at the Bay of Pigs to try to overthrow Castro. They failed, and relations between Cuba and the USA grew worse, while those between Cuba and the USSR grew closer.

The Missile Crisis

When the Cold War started, Truman decided to set up an organisation, the Central Intelligence Agency (CIA), to gather information by spying on the Russians. On 16 October 1962, CIA experts showed President Kennedy some photographs taken by one of their spy planes. One of these is shown in Source 32. The implications for the security of the US are shown in the map on page 129. Missiles based in Cuba, with a flight time of 17 minutes, could kill 80 million Americans.

How should Kennedy react? He had three options, apart from doing nothing (see Simulation). First, a nuclear attack on Cuba; second, a CONVENTIONAL attack on Cuba; third, a naval blockade of the island to prevent the missiles reaching their new bases. The whole world held its breath wondering if this was to be the beginning of a nuclear holocaust.

On 22 October Kennedy announced a naval blockade of Cuba. But how would Khrushchev react? What would happen when the ships carrying nuclear missiles on board (see Source 33) met US naval vessels? To everyone's relief the Russian ships stopped and turned round. So far, no war. But what about the bases on Cuba?

On the 26 and 27 October, Kennedy received two messages from Khrushchev, with rather different offers (see Source 34). Kennedy was uncertain how to react and the mood was tense (see Source 35). Then Robert Kennedy suggested responding to the offer of 26 October and ignoring that of 27th. Kennedy agreed to move his missiles from Turkey if all work in Cuba stopped. If not, the USA would invade Cuba. Again the world waited. On 28 October Khrushchev accepted Kennedy's offer. The crisis which brought the superpowers close to nuclear war was over.

▼ SOURCE 33
Missiles on the deck of a Russian transport ship on the way to Cuba.

◄ SOURCE 32
Photograph from a U2 spy-plane of a Russian missile base in Cuba, 1962. The labels were added by the US State Department.

SOURCE 34

(A) 'If assurances were given that the United States would not attack Cuba, and the blockade was lifted, the question of the missile sites on Cuba would be entirely different. We and you ought not to pull on the ends of the rope in which you have tied the knot of war, because the more the two of us pull, the tighter that knot will be tied.'

(B) 'You are worried by Cuba...because it is 90 miles from America, but Turkey is next to us. I therefore make this proposal. We agree to remove from Cuba...offensive means. The United States for its part will remove its means from Turkey.'

(Extracts of letters from Khrushchev to Kennedy:
(A) 26 October 1962; (B) 27 October 1962.)

SOURCE 35

There were arguments – sharp disagreements, everyone was tense – all were weighed down with worry. ...The President's mind went to other areas of the World. What was going to happen in Berlin and Turkey, if we attacked Cuba? We were deciding really for all mankind.

(Robert Kennedy, the President's brother, describes the tense atmosphere in the White House during the crisis.)

Simulation

Split the class into groups of five.

Each group is led by a person playing either Kennedy or Khrushchev.

The other four are advisers:

1 *Military expert.*

2 *Intelligence – how the other side thinks.*

3 *Diplomatic expert – negotiating with the other side.*

4 *Press – telling your version to your own people.*

There are three main crisis points:

16 October, when Kennedy is shown the photographs.

22 October, when the US blockade starts.

26 October, when the whole issue of bases in Cuba is discussed.

In each case each side should:

Consider all the options and their possible consequences for both sides.

For example, on 16 October Kennedy could choose:

A *Do nothing: makes him unpopular; gives Khrushchev a victory.*

B *Attack Cuba with nuclear weapons: would destroy sites; could lead to world nuclear war.*

C *Attack Cuba with conventional weapons: would destroy sites; could escalate to long war with US casualties.*

D *Naval blockade: a limited response – puts next move on the Russians but leaves sites intact. No loss of life.*

Try to avoid real war, and especially nuclear war. Play for time. But remember: you mustn't lose face or climb down.

After each decision your press adviser, with everyone's help, writes a statement explaining the decision and why it was taken.

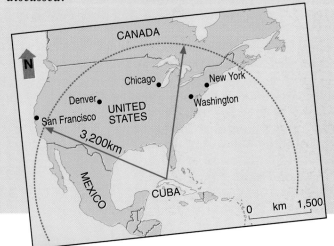

◄ Cuba and North America showing strike range of missiles fired from Cuba.

Conflict in Vietnam

What kind of sources do we have for this war? What effect did press reporting have on the people of the USA?

Vietnam was part of the French empire in Indo-China. During the Second World War, Ho Chi Minh, a Vietnamese communist, formed a resistance movement against the Japanese. For many Vietnamese, communism was a way of expressing their opposition to foreign rule, whether Japanese or French. Ho hoped for independence in 1945, but when the French rulers returned, he fought against them instead. In 1954 his experienced guerrilla commander, General Giap, inflicted a crushing defeat on the French at Dien Bien Phu.

French Indo-China became independent and was divided into four: North Vietnam, South Vietnam, Cambodia and Laos. Ho Chi Minh set up a communist government in North Vietnam and an anti-communist government took over in the South. Soon communists in the South, called the Vietcong, began to rebel. Ho sent them help and civil war began.

The USA had disapproved of French imperialism in 1945, but when communist China began to help Ho Chi Minh, US attitudes changed. They saw it as part of the struggle to prevent the spread of communism. The Truman Doctrine (see page 121) seemed to apply, and they gave help, first to the French, then to the South Vietnamese. The 'domino theory', shown in Source 36 explains their fears.

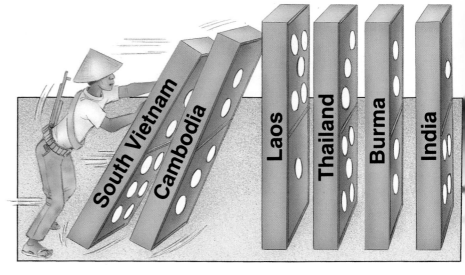

▲ **SOURCE 36**
The Domino Theory in East Asia. If one country falls to the communists, who will be next?

SOURCE 37

Most of the non-communist nations of Asia cannot, by themselves and alone, resist the growing might and grasping ambition of Asian communism.... An Asia so threatened by communist domination would imperil the security of the United States itself.

(President Johnson defends US policy in Vietnam.)

Escalation

By 1962, despite US help, the Vietcong were winning. President Kennedy decided to send in 16,500 US 'advisers'. His successor, President Johnson, was determined to win the war (see Source 37). By 1965 there were 180,000 US troops in Vietnam; by 1969 there were 500,000.

The huge technological might of the richest nation on earth was brought in. A greater tonnage of bombs was dropped on North Vietnam than were used in the entire Second World War (Source 38). But, as the British reporter James Cameron wondered: 'Would this sort of thing blow communism out of their heads?' In other words, in this war, unlike the Second World War, the USA was trying to win over the 'hearts and minds' of the enemy rather than destroying them.

▲ **SOURCE 38**
Bomb craters in Vietnamese paddy fields.

"You walk down a road between the rice paddies. There are Vietnamese in every paddy bent over working. None of them looks up when you pass. Then all of a sudden a mortar shell lands right in the middle of the patrol and a couple of guys you've been buddies with are dead and a couple of others are screaming in agony.

The Vietnamese are still working in the paddies just like they were, as though nothing at all had happened. Did one of them lob the mortar? If so which one? Should you kill all of them or some of them?

(US journalist Richard Hammer describes the feelings of US soldiers.)"

Defeat

The massive US effort was unsuccessful. Firstly, the Vietcong were a skilled GUERRILLA force with 20 years' experience. They mingled with local people by day and fought by night. They had underground command posts, with air-vents in hollow trees. They used bicycles to carry up to 220 kg of supplies along jungle tracks. US forces never found a way of dealing with this kind of opponent. Secondly, fighting a guerrilla war was hard for the soldiers (see Source 39). As James Cameron (opposite) suggests, the kind of war the US was fighting would not win over local people. Actions such as those shown and described in Sources 40 and 41 did the US cause no good with the Vietnamese people.

Thirdly, the US public saw pictures like Source 40 and read letters like Source 41. The war was costing them $30 billion a year and 300 American lives a week. A strong anti-war movement began.

Talks to end the war began in 1969 and the US began to pull troops out. Peace was signed in Paris in 1973. In 1975 the North Vietnamese conquered South Vietnam.

◄ **SOURCE 40**
Vietnamese woman suspected of being a member of the Vietcong, held by a US soldier. How can he tell whom she supports?

◄ **SOURCE 41**
Letter to a local paper in the USA, March 1967.

Dear Editor,

Here are portions of a letter I have received from my son who is now stationed in Vietnam.

"Dear Mum and Dad, Today we went on a mission and I am not very proud of myself, my friends or my country. We burned every hut in sight! [He goes on to describe how a soldier threw a grenade into a hut.] After he threw it and was running for cover we all heard a baby crying from inside the hut. There was nothing we could do.... After the explosion we found the mother, two children and an almost new-born baby. The fragile bodies were torn apart. Well Dad, you wanted to know what it's like here.... Does this give you an idea?"

Needless to say I was much disturbed to read this letter. I think the American people should understand what they mean when they advocate a continuation of our war effort in Vietnam.

A GI's Dad.

③ Target Questions

1 How useful is Source 37 for telling us about US motives in getting involved in Vietnam?

2 Which of Sources 38, 39, 40 and 41 are more useful for telling us: what the war was like for the Vietnamese? What the war was like for US soldiers?

3 What would you want to know about Source 39 in order to assess its reliability?

4 How useful is Source 41 for telling us about: the way the war was fought? Feelings about the war back in the USA?

5 Use all the sources to explain what you think the Vietnam war was like for both sides.

6 What other types of sources would you like to see to make your account in Question 5 more accurate?

SOURCE 42

There are more than 40,000 nuclear warheads in the world today. The total strength is about 1 million Hiroshima bombs. Every large bomb has a destructive strength greater than all explosions ever used since the discovery of gunpowder.

(UN Report on nuclear weapons, 1984.)

Time chart

1963

The 'Hot-Line'. Communication between Kennedy and Khrushchev in the Cuban Missile crisis (see page 128) had not been easy. The hot-line was a special telephone line between Moscow and Washington.
Test Ban Treaty banning nuclear weapons testing, signed by the USA, USSR and Britain.

1968

Nuclear Non-Proliferation Treaty – USA, USSR and Britain agree not to supply nuclear technology to other countries. Not signed by France, Japan, China, Israel and South Africa.
Vietnam: USSR and China supply North Vietnam with weapons, but not soldiers.

1970

By now US had 2,300 missiles and USSR 1,500. US developed M1RVs – Multiple independently targeted warheads.

1971

US and Chinese table-tennis teams meet for tournament. First contact between US and communist China for 22 years. China admitted to UN.

1972

President Nixon visits Mao Zedong in China.
SALT (Strategic Arms Limitation Talks). Both agree to stop building strategic nuclear weapons.

1975

Helsinki agreement between President Carter and Brezhnev, agrees to recognise existing borders in Europe. Russian and American cosmonauts meet in space.

1979

SALT 2 should have been signed in 1977 but was agreed nearly two years late. Then USSR invaded Afghanistan in 1979 and US Congress refused to ratify treaty.

1980

Election of President Reagan. US defence expenditure increased from $178 billion to $367 billion by 1986 in a new arms race. Western nations boycott Olympic Games held in Moscow.

1984

SDI (Strategic Defence Initiative) Reagan called this 'Star Wars' – the US plan to build an anti-missile system in space.
Cruise missiles deployed in Europe.

1985

Gorbachev becomes Soviet leader. Begins serious approach to peace talks.

1987

Gorbachev and Reagan agree INF (Intermediate Nuclear Forces) Treaty in Washington. Nuclear missiles withdrawn from Europe.

Détente and the end of the Cold War

Détente is a French word meaning an easing of tension. After the eyeball to eyeball confrontation of the Cuban Missile Crisis of 1962, the superpowers moved towards détente on several occasions. Détente could be:

1 cutting back on nuclear weapons,
2 not interfering in each other's affairs,
3 friendship between leaders on each side (summit meetings),
4 friendship at other levels: culture, sport, science and economics.

Why did the superpowers want détente?

The arms race had terrible dangers. With so many weapons on each side (see Source 42) there was always the danger of an accident. Even the testing of weapons created 'fall-out' which devastated parts of the Pacific (used by the USA) and Central Asia (used by the USSR).

The arms race was also expensive. Spending on weapons took money away that could have been used to improve the standard of living of ordinary people, especially in the USSR and China.

For the USA, détente with China and Russia prevented the two great communist powers from joining together. For the USSR, Khrushchev was the first to call for 'peaceful co-existence'. This was taken up by other Soviet leaders, such as Leonid Brezhnev (1966–1982). China wanted a major ally against the USSR after the split between China and Russia in 1960 (the Sino-Soviet split). Anti-war movements put pressure on governments to disarm (see Source 43).

▲ SOURCE 43
A demonstration by the Campaign for Nuclear Disarmament (CND).

Why was détente so difficult to achieve?

Both sides continued to be suspicious of each other. The bitter mistrust of the 1940s and 1950s continued. Some leaders were keen on détente, such as President Richard Nixon (president 1968 to 1974 – see Source 44). Others were not, such as President Ronald Reagan (president 1980 to 1988) who called the USSR 'an evil empire'.

How could you tell if the other side really had disarmed as agreed? This is called 'verification'. It would mean letting experts from the other side into your country to see what you had done. Neither side was keen on this.

New weapons were always being designed. For example, when the superpowers agreed to cut the number of missiles, each side invented new ones with more warheads per missile.

Now look at the list of events in the time chart opposite. Which are examples of détente? If so, which of the categories 1 to 4 at the top of the opposite page does it fall into? What were the motives of each side in that particular event? In which years was détente going well? When was it going badly?

▲ **SOURCE 44**
US President Nixon meets Chinese Chairman Mao Zedong in Peking in 1972.

◄ **SOURCE 45**
Reagan and Gorbachev meet in Iceland in 1986.

▲ **SOURCE 46**
Soviet nuclear missile being dismantled under terms of the INF Treaty.

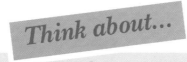

Why did the Cold War come to an end? What made the changes possible?

The end of the Cold War

President Gorbachev was serious about bringing major changes to the USSR. The cost of the arms race was crippling the USSR. For his policy of restructuring the economy (called *perestroika*) to work, there had to be peace. Gorbachev's other main policy was called *glasnost* (openness). One aspect of *glasnost* was developing trust with the West, so that proper verification of arms reduction was now possible.

Gorbachev pulled Soviet forces out of the long war in Afghanistan; he met Reagan in Reykjavik in 1986 (Source 45) and Washington in 1987 and negotiated disarmament, which was really carried out (see Source 46).

Gorbachev also allowed Eastern European countries to form their own governments, without sending in Soviet tanks to stop them as his predecessors had in 1956 (Hungary) and 1968 (Czechoslovakia) (see pages 126 and 127). In East Germany the government collapsed in 1989 and the Berlin Wall was breached. Although nuclear weapons still exist, the Cold War is really over.

How has the UN changed?

As we have seen, the UN was set up by the Great Powers at the end of the Second World War. The early meetings were attended only by the USA, Britain, USSR and China. With the addition of France, these made up the permanent members of the Security Council. The make-up of the UN therefore favoured the powerful countries of the world.

What was completely unforeseen, however, was the Cold War. The hostility between the USA and USSR was often played out in the UN. The original 51 members had an in-built bias towards the USA. They included 20 nations from the Americas, who invariably supported the USA, plus America's allies in Western Europe. The Russians reacted by using their veto to block the UN from doing anything positive. The organisation was often paralysed. This led to the 'Uniting for Peace' resolution of 1950 (Source 47).

In 1949, the communist government of the Mao Zedong took over in China, but the UN, led by the USA, refused to recognise it. It was only Russia's withdrawal from the Security Council in protest over this issue that made UN action in Korea possible (see pages 124 and 125). 'Uniting for Peace' was also used to send UN troops to the Suez Canal in 1956, despite the veto of Britain and France.

During the late 1950s and 1960s another change came to the UN, as Source 48 makes clear. The winning of independence by new nations in Africa and the Far East (see unit 6) increased the UN's size. It also eventually gave it a new majority, neither pro-USA nor pro-USSR. The Secretary-General from 1953 to 1961, Dag Hammarskjöld, energetically supported this new trend (see Source 50). This new group of states first used its influence in the crisis over the Congo in 1960, which led to the biggest UN action so far.

Look again at pages 118 and 119 about the setting up of the UN and the way it works. Now look at Source 48, which shows the first 51 members of the UN. Remember that there was a Cold War going on between the two superpowers from 1945 to 1989. Then talk about these questions in groups.

* *Which side in the Cold War had a majority of supporters in the Security Council in 1945? In the General Assembly?*

* *How did the Russians feel about this? What could they do about it?*

* *Suppose you were from a small country, not in the Security Council, nor a particular ally of the USA or USSR. How could you influence the UN?*

* *Look at Source 48. There are now 184 members. Why weren't they members in 1945? What do you think they would want from the UN?*

Use your answers to these questions to prepare for the target question.

SOURCE 47

I f the Security Council, because of lack of unanimity amongst its permanent members, fails to maintain peace and security, the General Assembly shall consider the matter immediately with a view to making appropriate recommendations to members including, in the case of a breach of the peace, or an act of aggression, the use of force.

(The 'Uniting for Peace' resolution, agreed by the UN in 1950. It could transfer decisions from the deadlocked Security Council to the General Assembly.)

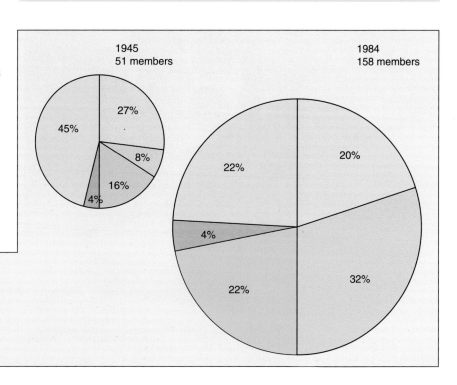

SOURCE 48 ▶
Membership of the UN, 1945 to present day.

Legend:
- Americas
- Europe
- Africa
- Asia
- Oceania

1945
51 members

1984
158 members

Intervention in the Congo

The Congo (since 1971 called Zaire), covers a huge area of Central Africa. It had originally been ruled by an independent Belgian company, who had developed it with great brutality. In 1908 it was taken over by the Belgian government who clearly intended to rule it for ever. No Africans were trained to be doctors, lawyers, engineers or army officers, or educated beyond primary level. The Belgians made huge profits from the copper mines in the south-east part of the country, called Katanga, and forced Africans to work in the mines. The country was therefore ill-prepared when it was suddenly given independence in 1960.

Within days the country was in a state of violent chaos. Congolese troops MUTINIED against their Belgian officers and began attacking Belgian civilians. The Belgian government, quite illegally, flew in their own paratroops to protect Belgian citizens. Then the rich province of Katanga declared its own independence. It had a black leader, Moïse Tshombe, but a white-led mercenary army paid for by the rich Belgian mining company. Who was really ruling Katanga?

The Congolese prime minister, Patrice Lumumba, called on the UN for help. Dag Hammarskjöld rapidly put together a large force of 20,000 soldiers, mainly from India, Ghana, Ireland, Canada and Nigeria (Source 49). The UN had to do the job the Belgians had failed to do in teaching the Congolese to run their own country. Courses were set up to train teachers, civil servants, police officers, telecommunication engineers, and so on. They had to deal with a near famine, as food supplies were disrupted by the war.

They also had to deal with a worsening civil war, as different groups struggled for power. Lumumba asked the UN to help him bring Katanga back into the Congo. But did the UN have the right to intervene in a civil war like this? Many Western nations supported Katanga and its business links. During the indecision Lumumba called on the USSR for aid, and it looked as if an international conflict could start in Africa. The African states now took the initiative. Dr Nkrumah of Ghana spoke against 'extending the Cold War to Africa' and said 'the UN must not let this happen'. The Katangese revolt was eventually ended, but

SOURCE 49
UN forces in action in the Congo, 1961.

SOURCE 50

It is not the Soviet Union, nor indeed any other big power, who need the United Nations for their protection; it is the others. I shall remain at my post in the interest of all those other nations, as long as they wish me to do so.

(Dag Hammarskjöld's reply to the request from Russian leader Khrushchev that he should resign, 1961.)

not before Lumumba had been deposed and then murdered in 1961 and Hammarskjöld killed in an air crash in the same year.

The UN had been fairly effective and appeared to have gained a new voice from the newly independent nations. But the problem of how the UN should deal with civil wars has remained, as in the former Yugoslavia since 1991, for example.

1 Target Question

How far had the UN changed by the 1960s?

In your answer you should consider what these changes were, what had not changed, and whether you think the change was for the better.

How does poverty affect the environment?

The issues dealt with in these last three pages are often covered in geography lessons. But there is a historical aspect to environmental problems too, as we shall see on these pages.

We can tell if a person is poor (see unit 1), but how do you tell if a country is poor? One way to do this is to take the total wealth of the country and divide it by the number of people:

$$\frac{\text{Gross National Product (GNP)}}{\text{Population}} = \text{per capita GNP}$$

Source 51 shows the per capita GNP of eight of the Least Developed Countries (LDCs) and of the UK, for comparison. Source 52 shows the 31 LDCs in the world.

Source 51 also shows some of the effects of poverty: poor countries cannot afford to pay teachers or build schools. Children of poor people cannot go to school because they have to work. High illiteracy means unskilled people, unable to break out of poverty. Poverty also means poor health. Poor people die young, as Source 51 shows. In 34 LDCs more than one child in four dies before the age of 5. Ill people cannot work, so they stay poor and cannot buy medical care.

Country	Per capita GNP 1983	Per cent illiterate	Life expectancy
Bangladesh	130	74	40-50
Benin	290	72	40-50
Botswana	920	59	40-50
Ethiopia	140	87	c.40
Haiti	320	79	40-50
Laos	805	6	50-60
Tanzania	290	26	40-50
North Yemen	510	73	c.40
UK	9,050	c.10	70+

The causes of poverty

As Source 52 shows, many LDCs are in hot countries. Hot damp climates breed disease. Hot dry climates (deserts) cannot grow crops.

World population has increased at an enormous rate this century. In 1900 it was about 1.5 billion (1,500,000,000), in 1987 it was 5 billion and by 2000 it will be 6 billion. The rate of increase is falling now, but it is the poorest countries, and the poorest families, who have the most children.

More people means more trees are cut down for fuel (half the people in the world depend on firewood for fuel). It means more farming, more grazing animals and so more land exhaustion. North Africa was once the main supplier of wheat to the Roman empire; now overgrazing and deforestation have turned most of it into desert areas.

▲ **SOURCE 51**
Table comparing 8 LDCs with the UK.

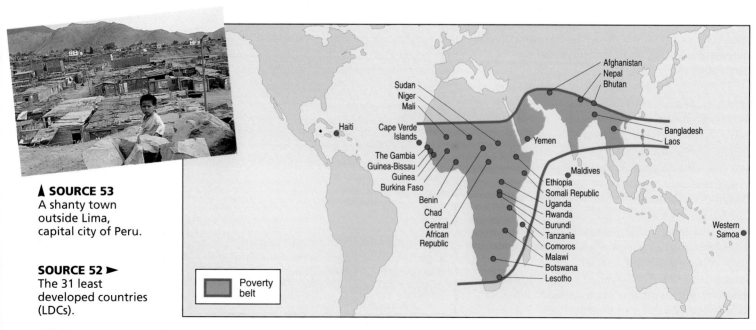

▲ **SOURCE 53**
A shanty town outside Lima, capital city of Peru.

SOURCE 52 ▶
The 31 least developed countries (LDCs).

Poverty belt

In many poor countries people have abandoned the countryside to make their lives in cities. Huge shanty towns have grown up (see Source 53). These take up farmland and cause huge pollution problems.

How does wealth affect the environment?

Rich countries, with 22 per cent of the world's population, consume 88 per cent of the world's mineral resources, 82 per cent of the world's energy and produce 86 per cent of the world's manufactured goods. Even so, huge amounts of these minerals, energy and manufacturing resources are wasted (Source 54).

Industry produces wealth, and a high standard of living for the people, but also creates much more pollution. One example of the results of a government which was determined to industrialise (see page 40) and to ignore the effects of pollution on people can be seen today in the former Soviet Union (Source 55). London used to have smoky fogs – smogs; in 1952 a few days of smog killed 4,000 people. California has acid fog. In both cases governments have acted to improve the environment.

Industrial pollution can have effects beyond the country that produces it, even to the whole planet. Acid rain, for example, is caused by industry in Britain and Western Europe and destroys forests and lakes in Scandinavia. The hole in the ozone layer, endangering life on the whole planet, is produced by CFC gases, used in aerosols, fridges, air-conditioners and in making hamburger cartons. All these products are almost exclusively used in the wealthy countries.

Nuclear power

Wealthy countries use a lot of energy. One way of producing this is to harness the heat created by a nuclear reaction to boil water to make steam to drive a turbine. The first country to build a reactor to use nuclear power in this peaceful way was the USSR in 1954. Britain's first reactor was opened in 1956. There are now 300 reactors in the world and some countries are heavily dependent on nuclear power: 65 per cent of France's electricity and 53 per cent of Taiwan's, for example, comes from nuclear power (Britain 20 per cent).

◄ SOURCE 55
Heavy industry in Dneprodzerzhinsk, in the former USSR.

SOURCE 54 ►
Car dump, Japan.

NUCLEAR POWER	
Arguments for:	**Arguments against:**
1 Coal, oil and other fossil fuels will run out. Using nuclear power will help conserve the reserves of these fossil fuels.	**1** Nuclear power has never been cheap. Building reactors is very expensive; so is 'de-commissioning' them (closing them down).
2 Burning coal creates acid rain and the 'greenhouse effect', warming the atmosphere, causing climatic change and changes in the sea level.	**2** We don't need that much energy. Alternatives, especially 'renewables' such as wind and tidal power should be used.
3 Nuclear power will be cheap. Although building a nuclear reactor is very expensive, once it is working the cost of the electricity it produces is very cheap.	**3** Nuclear power stations produce the material for nuclear weapons.
	4 Nuclear power stations only last 30 years but produce radioactive waste, which will continue to be dangerous for thousands of years.
	5 Accidents can have horrific results. The one in 1986 at Chernobyl, in the Ukraine, polluted a huge area and made animals as far afield as Cumbria and Lapland unfit to eat.

Rich and poor

In 1980 the Brandt Report was published. It pointed out that 'the gap between rich and poor countries is so wide that at the extremes people live in different worlds'. Often it is a gap between the fed and the hungry (Source 51).

When LDCs were colonies the imperial power controlled what crops should be grown and how they should trade. Now they are independent (see unit 6), but their economic position is the same. Many LDCs are dependent on selling one product to the rich countries (for example cocoa from Ghana, or copper from Zambia). If the price they receive falls, they are ruined. At the same time farming is distorted by having to grow more cash crops.

This system has been called neo-colonialism (see page 99). The relationship can affect the environment in poorer countries. For example, in the last few years the jungle of the Amazon basin in South America has been cut down at a great rate – 166,000 sq km in 1987 alone. This is to provide timber for paper and furniture and to clear space to graze beef cattle. In all cases, the products will go to the rich countries.

As we have seen on page 119, the UN tries to redress the balance. UNESCO tries to break the cycle of illiteracy by providing schools. The FAO tries to help poor farmers who cannot improve their farming techniques. UNCTAD tries to improve the terms of trade. The UN suggests that rich nations should give 0.7 per cent of their

▲ **SOURCE 51**
Cartoon in the *Observer*, July 1985. Food surpluses in Europe, starvation in LDCs.

▲ **SOURCE 52**
Woman farmer in India with a huge modern power station in the background. How is she helped by this industry?

SOURCE 53

Description of the effects of one particular aid scheme in India.

'In one project a power plant was built on land that formerly belonged to small farmers. Most families were compensated for the loss of their homes and given a place in a new housing estate. These lack even basic amenities and some homes flood regularly. From 267 families only 70 people found jobs in the power plant, and these are unskilled menial tasks.'

annual income as aid. In 1987 Norway gave 1 per cent, Britain 0.34 per cent, USA 0.24 per cent.

Many individuals in rich countries are generous: in 1984 in the UK Oxfam collected £24 million; Save the Children £16.5 million; Christian Aid £11 million and CAFOD £6 million. Some aid schemes are well thought out, helping people to become self-reliant rather than dependent, but some are not (see Sources 52 and 53). World inequality and threats to the environment need world-scale co-operation. The Brundtland Report, 1989, and the Rio Environmental Summit in 1992 tried to achieve this. Politicians, however, usually have to think in terms of their own nation, and have only short-term aims, while the problems need long-term solutions.

Anti-semitic
Prejudiced against Jews.

Apartheid
The policy of separate, and unequal, treatment of blacks and whites in South Africa.

Borstals
A place where offenders aged 15 to 21 are sent instead of prison.

Bourgeoisie
The people who own factories, banks or other business activities, or who live off the profit from investing their wealth in business or trade.

Boycott
Refusal to have any contact, commercial, artistic or sporting, with another country or person.

Bureaucrats
Powerful government officials.

Capitalism
The way of organising the economy of a country in which business, trade and industry are owned and run by investors who put money into these enterprises in the expectation of profit.

Civil rights
The personal rights and freedoms of each citizen.

Civil war
War between different groups of people within a country.

Coalition government
Government made up of the members of more than one party.

Collectivisation
In the USSR in the 1930s individual peasant holdings were joined together into one large unit, the collective farm or 'Kolkhoz'. The state ran the collective, took its share of the crop and the peasants then received their share according to how much work they had done.

Colonial
Colonies are the lands ruled by an *imperial* power.

Communists
Followers of Karl Marx who believe that the state should own all industries and economic enterprises and run them for the benefit of working people.

Constituencies
Divisions of the country, each of which elects one Member of Parliament.

Conventional
Ordinary; conventional weapons are non-nuclear weapons.

Democracy
A political organisation in which the government is made up of elected representatives.

Democratic (US politics)
One of the two main US political parties, the Democrats have traditionally had closer links with trade unions, the poor and ethnic minorities.

Denomination
A division or group within the Christian Churches.

Dictatorship
Rule by one person.

Diphtheria
A contagious, often fatal, disease which causes fever and breathing difficulties.

Discrimination
Treating people differently for some single reason, such as their age, skin colour or gender.

Disestablished
The Church of England is the Established Church, so it has close links with the state. A disestablished church, as in Wales, does not have these links.

Dissident
Someone who opposes the government, or its laws or its way of ruling.

Elite
A specially selected group, with more power, rights and privileges than the rest of society.

Evacuee
Someone who has been evacuated, that is, sent away from an area threatened with danger, such as British cities at the beginning of the Second World War.

Fascist
Extreme right-wing nationalist political group, hostile to *socialism, communism*, liberalism and in favour of one-party dictatorship.

Franchise
A group of people with the right to vote.

Guerrilla
Someone who fights a war in an unconventional way, avoiding open conflict.

Holocaust
The systematic attempt by the *Nazis* and their followers to exterminate the Jewish people.

Ideological
Motivated by beliefs rather than practicalities.

Immigrant
Someone who moves to another area or country to live and work there.

Imperial
Belonging to an empire. An empire consists of several states or areas ruled by one stronger state.

Laissez-faire
A government policy to do as little as possible to interfere in, or regulate, people's lives.

Missionaries
People of one religion who go out, often to another country, to convert people to their beliefs.

Munitions
Weapons of war.

Mutiny
The refusal of members of the armed forces to obey their officers.

Nationalise
The term used in Britain for the government taking over and running a business or industry.

Nazis
Members of the National Socialist German Workers' Party which governed Germany from 1933 to 1945.

Nonconformist
Members of Protestant churches which are not in the Church of England.

Ordination
The ceremony in which someone becomes a priest.

Paramilitary
Like a military organisation, with, for example, uniforms, ranks, drill and obedience to orders.

Peers
Members of the House of Lords.

Persecution
Attack on the *civil rights* of a person or group.

Pogrom
Attacks on the lives and *civil rights* of Jews in Russia in the late 19th century.

Proletariat
The Marxist term for working people, whose only economic asset is their work.

Propaganda
Information which gives a biased view of events or personalities, either by exaggeration, by omitting part of the story or by deliberate untruths.

Purges
Removing numbers of people from their jobs on the grounds that they are disloyal.

Referendum
Asking all citizens to express their view on a particular issue by voting on it.

Reparations
Financial payment made by one country to another after a war to repay them for the costs of the war.

Repatriated
Returned to a person's country of origin.

Republicans
One of the main parties in US politics. The Republicans have traditionally been linked to business and conservative interests.

Shares
In a capitalist system, a business enterprise will issue shares in order to raise money. People with money to invest will buy shares, expecting to make money from selling them at a higher price.

Socialist
A belief in the need for the state to intervene in economic affairs to protect weaker members of society from the exploitation of stronger members.

Stakhanovism
Stakhanov (page 41) was given special privileges and made an example for other workers. Stakhanovism was the extension of this policy to other workers.

Stock exchange
A place where people meet to buy and sell *shares*.

Suffrage
The right to vote.

Suffragettes
Members of the WSPU, the militant organisation which campaigned for women's *suffrage*.

Suffragists
Members of the NUWSS which campaigned for women's *suffrage* by peaceful means.

Superpower
An extremely powerful state.

Syndicalism
The theory that *capitalism* could be overthrown by workers in trade unions acting together to bring the country to a halt through a general strike.

Unorthodox
Unusual.

Veto
The right of a member of an organisation to forbid any of its actions from taking place.

Viceroy
The person who ruled India on behalf of the British monarch, who was also Emperor of India.

INDEX

ACKNOWLEDGEMENTS

Every effort has been made to contact the holders of copyright material but if any have been inadvertently overlooked, the publishers will be pleased to make the necessary arrangements at the first opportunity.

The publishers would like to thank the following for permission to reproduce photographs on these pages:

T = top, B = bottom, C = centre, L = left, R = right.

Aerofilms Limited 25; Allsport 88T; Apple Corps Ltd 68; Archiv für Kunst und Geschichte, Berlin 4B; Associated Press 98, 131; Barnaby's Picture Library 64R, 65T; BBC 97; Bede Gallery, Jarrow 42; Bettmann Archive 37; Blackpool Borough Council 72T; Bodleian Library, Oxford 33, 36T; The British Library 12, 36B, 90; Courtesy Butlins 46/47; Cymdeithas yr laith Gymraeg 88C; D.P.A. Manchester 20T; EMI Music Archive 27; Environmental Picture Library/ Derek Henderson 138R; Express Newspapers 81, 113, 118C; Peter Fisher 80; Format/ Ulrike Preuss 63; John Frost 46C; GLC Photo Library 11; Robert Harding Picture Library 137C; HM The Queen/ Royal Archives, Windsor Castle 6; Hulton Deutsch Collection © 3L&R, 5L, 7, 14, 15, 16B, 17, 18T, 20B, 21, 23, 24, 29, 31, 34T, 43, 45TL, 45B, 47B, 50, 52B, 53L, 54R, 55T, 56T, 57, 59T, 60, 64L, 65L&R, /Bettmann Archive 67L, 71, 76, 77T, 78, 79, 83C, 91, 93, 94R, 99, 100, 101, 102, 103, 104, 107, 108 109, 117, 118T, 122B, 124, 127C, 128, 132, 133T, 135; Illustrated London News Picture Library 18B; Imperial War Museum, London 30, 61T, 120, 125; Alan Jackson 47C; KAL/ Cartoonists' and Writers' Syndicate 138L; Library of Congress 24/25; Liverpool Record Office and Local History Department/ Hulton Deutsch Collection 8/9; London Transport Museum 22T, 72B; David Low/ Solo Syndication/ C.S.C.C./ University of Kent at Canterbury 45TR, 51; Magnum Photos 127B; Mary Evans Picture Library/ Fawcett Library 19; Museum für Gestaltung, Zürich 41; Museum of Labour History 32; Museum of London/ Bridgeman Art Library 10; NASA/ Science Photo Library 74B; National Library of Ireland 83TL&R, 83BR; National Maritime Museum, London 4T; National Museum of American Art, Smithsonian Institution, Transfer from the US Department of Labor 38; Robert Opie Collection 8L, 22B, 46B; Panos Pictures 75R; Popperfoto 5R, 61B, 74T 126; Press Association 28B, 34B; Punch Publications 13, 28T, 62, 85; Retrograph Archive/ Martin Breese 3T, 67R; Reuters/ Hulton Deutsch Collection 115R; Rex Features 53R, 69, 70, 73, 95C, 130; Science Photo Library 114; Scottish Fisheries Museum Trust 16T; Frank Spooner Pictures 54L, 55B, 75L 86, 87, 92, 115L, 116 133C&B, 136, 137T; Sporting Pictures 77R; Tesco Stores PLC 94L;Courtesy of Time Magazine 44; Topham Picture Source 48, 49, 56B, 122C; Tower Hamlets Central Library 58/59; Ullstein Bilderdienst 39; United Nations/ Hulton Deutsch Collection 118B; Vogue, Condé Nast Publications Limited 66; Reg Wilson 95T.

Cover photograph: Sally & Richard Greenhill.

The authors and publishers gratefully acknowledge the following publications from which written sources in this book are drawn:

Extracts reproduced from *All Our Working Lives*, Peter Pagnamenta and Richard Overy with the permission of BBC Enterprises Limited; Jonathan Cape Ltd for an extract from *Never Again*, Peter Hennessey; Child Poverty Action Group for an extract from *Hardship Britain: Being Poor in the 1990s*, Ruth Cohen et al., CPAG Ltd, 1992; Milly Donbrow and Gateshead Libraries and Arts for an extract from *They Docked at Newcastle and Wound up in Gateshead*; Victor Gollancz Ltd for an extract from *One Day in the Life of Ivan Denisovich*, Alexander Solzhenitsyn, translated by Ralph Parker © 1963; HMSO for an extract from *Board of Trade Journal, 1948* and an extract from *Report of the Equal Opportunities Commission*, 1978; © Times Newspapers Ltd 1992 for an extract from 'Ordination of Women Priests', Ruth Gledhill (*The Times* 12.11.1992); Warner Brothers Inc. for the lyrics of 'The Times They Are A-Changin'' © 1963; an extract from *The Fifties*, Neil Thompson, 1991, reproduced by permission of Watts Books, a division of the Watts Publishing Group.

First published in 1994 by Collins Educational
77- 85 Fulham Palace Road
Hammersmith
London
W6 8JB
Reprinted 1996
ISBN 0 00 327268 0

Edited by Helen Mortimer and Lorimer Poultney
Series planned by Nicole Lagneau
Cover designed by Peartree Design Associates
Book designed by Peartree Design Associates
Picture research by Anna Calvert (Hulton Deutsch Collection), Celia Dearing, Diana Morris and Suzanne Williams
Production by Mandy Inness
Artwork by Hardlines pages 26, 29, 36, 66, 70, 71, 89, 111, 134; Jillian Luff pages 27, 96, 98, 105, 120, 122, 129, 136; Julia Osorno pages 80, 119, 129, 130
Printed By HarperCollins Publishers Hong Kong